The Story of

J. C. Tregarthen

Alpha Editions

This edition published in 2024

ISBN : 9789362927682

Design and Setting By
Alpha Editions
www.alphaedis.com
Email - info@alphaedis.com

As per information held with us this book is in Public Domain.
This book is a reproduction of an important historical work. Alpha Editions uses the best technology to reproduce historical work in the same manner it was first published to preserve its original nature. Any marks or number seen are left intentionally to preserve its true form.

Contents

PREFACE ....- 1 -

CHAPTER I EARLY TROUBLES ....- 2 -

CHAPTER II EDUCATION ....- 12 -

CHAPTER III INDEPENDENCE ....- 20 -

CHAPTER IV CHASED BY POLECATS.................................- 27 -

CHAPTER V A DELUSIVE REFUGE ....- 32 -

CHAPTER VI BACK ON CARN BREA ....- 37 -

CHAPTER VII FROM PILLAR TO POST ....- 45 -

CHAPTER VIII THE GREAT WINTER ....- 55 -

CHAPTER IX PERIL OF DEATH ....- 63 -

CHAPTER X THE FIENDS OF THE WILD ....- 74 -

CHAPTER XI L'HOMME S'AMUSE ....- 84 -

PREFACE

Whilst few, if any, animals have more enemies than the hare, none perhaps is better endowed with instincts to outwit them.

As that great mediæval hunter, the Master of Game, said in 1402: "There is no man in this world that would say that any hound can unravel that which a hare has done, or that could find her. For she will go the length of a bowshot or more by one way, and ruse again by another and then she will take her way by another side and the same she shall do ten, twelve or twenty times, then she will come into some hedge or thicket and shall make semblance to abide there and then will make crosswards ten or twelve times and will make her ruses and then she will take some false path and shall go thence a great way, and such semblance she will make many times before she goes to her seat."

Shifts such as these, probably unrivalled in their subtlety, are embodied in the incidents, based on observation or record, which make up the present story of the hare, a story for the first time told at length.

Imagination has of necessity supplied much of the description of a life spent under the stars; but nothing alien to the hare's habits and character has been wittingly introduced, though what the outlook on the world, what the thoughts of this and the predatory creatures entering into the drama are, must ever remain a matter for speculation.

The narrative has been placed a century back, chiefly because the more primitive days of a bygone Cornwall allowed the inclusion of more numerous fauna, and permitted the use of a wilder setting.

For my aim has been to present a picture instinct with the spirit of the wild, of the upland, moor, and cliff of the Land's End at a time when the prey and the beast of prey roamed the night fearless of snare and gin—and man rarely intruded by day—under conditions, rapidly fading into oblivion, which seem worthy of record before they disappear for ever.

J. C. T.

ROSMORRAN, NEWQUAY,

    CORNWALL, *Aug. 28, 1912.*

CHAPTER I
EARLY TROUBLES

The Cornish Heights terminate near the Land's End in four wild hills of singular charm, though of very modest altitude. Springing as they do from a treeless tableland, they look quite like a miniature mountain range, especially when seen through rolling mists or capped by the rain-laden clouds which, like birds coming weary from the Atlantic, settle on their summits. Man seldom intrudes there, though they offer a peerless prospect over promontory and ocean. The faint paths amongst ling and furze are not his: they have been traced by the foxes that kennel on this silent retreat, or by badgers going to and from the deep sett on the northern slope; for the desolate upland has long been given over to the outlawed creature, and furnished sanctuary to any wildling that sought it.

To these hills, in the late winter of a year long ago, there came a hare in search of a spot to which she might safely commit her young. She was hard to satisfy, rejecting for this reason or for that a score of harbourages that competed for her favour. One night she all but decided on a bramble-patch near the top of Caer Bran; the next she fancied first a heathery knoll on Bartinney, then an abandoned mine-heap on Sancreed Beacon; and at the last moment rejected both for the western slope of Chapel Carn Brea, partly on account of its uninterrupted outlook, but more because it was less overrun than the sister hills by the predatory creatures that infested the countryside. All through the month of March she had not seen a polecat or even a stoat upon the hillside; only once had she detected on it the trail of an enemy; so with a feeling of security the timorous mother entrusted her young to its keeping, laying them in a tussock of coarse grass near a ruined chantry.

They were pretty little things with wide-open eyes, distinguishable by only the white star in the forehead of the male and the greater restlessness that he displayed. The tiny fellow, as if eager to explore the world into which he had just been born, was all agog to be out and about in the afterglow, and had not his mother checked him till the impulse passed, he would have left the form and perhaps lost himself amongst the furze. He constantly renewed his struggles to have his way; but the moment he ceased, she removed the restraining pad and caressed him till, like his sister, he became drowsy and at length fell asleep.

When the stars shone bright, the hare rose, stretched her stately limbs, covered the little sleepers with the grass-blades, gathered herself for a spring, and leapt to an outcropping rock. On landing she leapt again and again and again, in order to prevent any beast of prey from following her tracks and discovering the form. After taking these precautions she made for the crest of the hill, and standing on the ruin, snuffed the wind and scrutinised the waste. Presently, assured that no enemy threatened, she set out for the feeding-ground. At the foot of the long slope she repeated her ruse of the leaps, and passed through a hole in the wall that separated the wild from the farm land, to which she had been attracted by the tender herbage of the young wheat.

Near midnight the leverets awoke and found her gone; yet in their loneliness they uttered neither plaint nor call, nor, strange to say, attempted to leave the form, but nestled close hour after hour awaiting her return. They gave no heed to the wind, for its sighing meant nothing to them; but at early dawn, though no sound broke the silence, the cocked ears first of one, then of the other, told they were all expectation for some signal. Soon there came the faint, low call which instinct whispered was their mother's, followed by the soft beat of the pads, growing more and more distinct till with a last bound the hare cleared the wide space between the rock and the form, and at once gave herself to the hungry, excited mites. Whilst she suckled them, a lark rose and greeted the day with notes so rapturous as to drown the crowings of the cocks in the homesteads dotting the plain. The leverets fed and fed till they were satisfied, then settled down to rest against their mother's side, where presently the sun, risen above Caer Bran, discovered them, and threw a bright splash of warm light across their russet coats.

C. Reid.]   [*To face p. 4.*

"THEY NESTLED CLOSE."

It was a lovely April morning. Towards noon a big black cloud came up out of the west bringing needed rain, whilst a rainbow arched land and sea; and then the first call of the cuckoo rang out through the stillness. Chapel Carn Brea faintly echoed "Cuckoo! Cuckoo!" The joyous notes brought the housewife to the door, checked the frolics of the wondering lambs, made the field-mice sit up and listen and the leverets prick their waking ears. The far-flung message that told of kindly weather and plenty for man and beast cheered every living thing that heard it: it cheered even the hare as she sat and watched over her young, full of misgivings for their safety. Their helplessness, still more her own powerlessness to defend them against enemies, stirred her deepest feelings, and made her mothering instinct so much stronger than that of the vixen laid up with cubs in the croft beyond the wheatfield. She was haunted by the dread of being bereft of them; and incapable of defence though she was, her fears kept her ever alert and vigilant. She never slept. Even when she drowsed her open, wakeful eyes saw all that passed within their range—the farmer faring to his work and hastening to his meals, the cows driven to and from the fields, the pigs wandering up and down the lane, the donkey browsing on the furzy waste by the common with the large pool, and the geese who, towards sunset, waddled from it to the farmyard gate cackling to be penned, as if apprehensive of being carried off by the hill-foxes that came and sniffed at their door when man was abed. She noted too the ravens as they winged by on their way to the cliffs, and the kites as they soared high overhead; she watched with no little concern the buzzard whose shadow passed over her as he searched the hillside before alighting on the broken chancel of the ruin. His terrifying cat-like mew caused the leverets to stir beneath her, but she herself remained as motionless as the furze; indeed, till the sun had set, she never moved for fear of prying eyes.

Four days passed without disquieting incident, but on the fifth the vixen paid a visit to the hill and threw the hare into a fever of anxiety. The daring marauder came at high noon, during the farmer's dinner-hour, when the land is forsaken and the peace of the waste spreads to the fields, enticing the nocturnal prowler to venture forth in broad daylight in search of food. Thus lured, the vixen, yielding to the importunities of her hungry cubs, stole from her earth and, keeping to the overgrown ditches, gained the boundary wall without exposing herself to view. But the instant her mask showed above the coping-stone the hare espied her, and from that moment followed every movement. She thought that the fox knew of her presence and was in search of her, as well as she might, for the hill harboured no prey save herself and her young, at least none worth the coming for. So while the vixen searched the lower slopes the hare watched with eyes starting from her head, anxious to learn whether the murderous creature would hit the line she had left at early dawn. Once she crossed it without checking; she flashed over it again near the Giant's Bowl, and then the hare knew that the trail would not betray her; the hot sun had evaporated every particle of what little scent she had left.[1] The hunter moved at an unusually quick pace, as if she had set herself the task of examining the whole hillside during the short time that man remained within doors. Now she threaded the bushes, now she leapt them; once she was lost to view in a patch of tall furze gorgeous with blossom, but in a few seconds she reappeared at the far end to continue the quest in the open. At last near the black shadow cast by a boulder she stopped, assumed a listening attitude, then plunged her long nose into a bush after a mouse, but apparently without getting it, for she did not lick her chops. Nothing disconcerted, however, on she went again, ranging to and fro without a pause till, half-way up the slope, she stood suddenly still and looked towards the homestead as if all at once alive to the risk she was running. A glance satisfied her that man was still indoors, and again she resumed the quest, if possible with greater keenness than before. Every stride now was taking her dangerously nearer and nearer to the hare, but whilst she was yet some five or six rods below the form a sheep-dog barked, and in an instant she was transformed from a lithe hunter into a craven creature. Crouching, she fixed her gaze on the dog expressing his delight at the reappearance of his master, who stood in shirt-sleeves at the open door. "Down, Shep." At the sound of the man's voice the vixen sank into the herbage as if turned to lead, and remained there motionless, save in heaving flank and lolling tongue. Presently the farmer withdrew; the vixen slunk down the hill, carefully avoiding the exposed places, climbed the wall, and vanished from sight.

Much as the hare was relieved by this retreat, she could not regain her peace of mind; for the visit left her with the fear that the creature would return at nightfall and renew the search, a thought which urged her to remove the leverets at dusk. But where? The nearest spot that commended itself to her was at the foot of Bartinney, about a mile distant; and the way thither led across the trails of fox and badger, who might surprise her with her burden, and have her at their mercy. Her position was a very difficult one; to stay was perilous, to shift was no less so. Uncertain what to do for the best, she remained irresolute till the stars began to peep; then, hoping against hope that the fox might not come after all, she decided to remain. In any case she must go and feed, yet setting-out time came and went whilst the hare kept to the form. She could not tear herself away from her young with this danger hanging over them. A sickle moon lit hill and plain and threw into relief the coping-stone of the wall on which the eyes of the anxious mother were fixed. Against the granite she could not fail to see the dark form of her enemy. The better to observe, the hare raised herself on her hind legs; and the leverets, thinking she was going to play with them, stood up too, resting their forefeet against her sides; but at a whisper from their mother they sank down again into a sitting posture. The night wore on, however, without sign of the fox, and at length the hare, feeling somewhat reassured, set out for the nearest feeding-ground. There she browsed until midnight, when apprehension for her young drove her back to the hill. Although she found all well, she stayed close by and fed on the rough herbage near the summit. When she returned to the form her fears had nearly subsided; by dusk they no longer haunted her, and in a day or two she dismissed the fox from her mind.

She thought that her enemy, satisfied that the hill was bare of prey, would not trouble her again, so that it came as a surprise when, a few mornings later, she espied a vixen at the foot of the slope, endeavouring to solve the puzzle of the scent the hare had left on her way to the form less than an hour before. It was strange how little the sight perturbed her, but when unaffected by her extreme anxiety for the leverets she knew from experience there was no real need for fear. Never once had she known a fox to succeed in tracing her from foiled ground, though in the past she had known many who had tried as the vixen was now trying. There near the wall the creature persisted in the almost hopeless task, following now this way, now that along the many lines of scent to discover the final course taken by the hare after her last leap. Over and over again she seemed on the point of giving it up: the network of trails maddened and bewildered her; and her irritation made her snap viciously at the long bramble spray in which her brush got entangled. Presently, in her despair, she made a cast at random; as luck would have it, she hit the true line. At once she was all alive; her brush, which had hung lifeless, now wagged furiously, and at the sight of her enemy's success the hare grew uneasy. Slowly, very slowly, the vixen advanced along the trail as if fearful of losing what had cost her so much trouble to find. Anon she came to the place above the clump of blossoming furze where since the midday visit the hare had woven another maze of tracks before coming to the leaping-place by the form. On reaching it the vixen tried to follow the trail as it had been laid, but the criss-crossing it had received so confused her that presently she lost patience and made a short cast beyond. Here she happened on a part of the trail where the hare had returned on her foil, and on coming to the spot near the ruin where it ended she actually raised her mask as if she believed the hare had taken wing and might be seen in mid-air. For a moment she seemed to despair again; but the hunger caused by the night's bad hunting and the thought of her five ravenous cubs goaded her on; she shook the dew from her coat and made another cast. This took her within a dozen yards of the spot where mother and young squatted flat on the ground. It seemed that the vixen must scent them; had there been a breath of wind she could hardly have failed; but the air was still; not a spray or blade moved save those disturbed by the vixen as she moved hither and thither with ears widespread to catch the slightest sound. A stifled cry, the faintest rustle in that silence must have betrayed them; through the trying, critical seconds, however, they never moved, they scarcely breathed.

The vixen seemed loath to leave the spot; but at length she quitted it for the summit, where she searched the fallen stones and scaled the crumbled walls, her form clearly outlined against the sky now tinted with orange by the coming day. On the stone lintel she presently came to a stand, arrested by the sight of the sun which peeped above the eastern hills and warned her that it was time to be seeking her earth. Reluctant as she was to obey, she dropped to the ground and made her way slowly down the shadowed slope. Half-way in the descent she suddenly turned her mask and scrutinised the ground in the hope of catching the hare with head raised watching her retreat; but bush, rock, and frond alone met her roving eyes. Near the Giant's Bowl she again looked back, and by the expression on her face, now vindictive rather than perplexed, seemed to say: "Wily one, you've beaten me this dawn, but I'll lick my chops over you yet, both you and your tender young ones." Then, the rumble of wheels urging her, she hurried away, her beautiful coat all aripple with the play of her lissom limbs. As soon as she had crossed the wall, the hare, who had observed her from behind the blades, resumed the suckling of her frightened young, fondling them as she had never done before.

It had been a narrow escape, and the hare was now all impatience to forsake the hill. But that could not be before nightfall, so she and the leverets spent the long day unnerved by the rank scent left by the fox on the herbage. The slow sun at last sank beneath the sea. At once the hare took the doe leveret in her mouth and carried it along the southern flank of the chain for more than a mile to the foot of Bartinney, where she laid it in a patch of bracken bordering a little green. The next moment she was on her way back at her best pace, as though she dreaded that the vixen might forestall her. But no enemy was to be seen: the jack was as she had left him. Seizing him by the skin of the neck she bore him rapidly along despite his kicking, crouching whilst two stoats passed, dropping him thrice to rest herself, and finally depositing him in a clump of rushes by a rill some score yards from his sister. It was not without a reason that she laid them on opposite sides of the green, for by thus separating them she hoped that at least one might escape detection in the event of a visit from an enemy.

On collecting himself after his strange experience, the jack sat and listened to the music of the water, whilst through an opening in the rushes his eyes scanned the green, whose close velvety sward seemed to cry aloud to be gambolled on. There, so the country people aver, the fairies forgather to hold high revel on the inviting turf, tripping to the tinkling of the falls, in the dark-green ring lighted by innumerable glow-worms. No little folk appeared that night, however; nothing in fact came near until the hare returned to attend to her young, before vanishing like the wraith she seemed and ensconcing herself in some brambles on the lip of the green.

She had not been there long when a magpie left his resting-place in the hawthorn overhanging the turf and stood preening his feathers on the topmost spray. Presently, his quick eyes noted the marks left by the hare's pads on the dewy surface, and examined them searchingly as if to learn the identity of the trespasser. He imagined that a badger or a fox had made them; the thought that a hare—he had only seen one—had crossed the green never entered his head, much less that a family of hares was at that moment lying hidden around it. The inquisitive bird was soon joined by his mate, and after a little chatter he flew away with her towards a homestead from which the smoke was just beginning to rise. They alighted on the elder-tree springing from the wall of the rickyard, the white of their plumage very conspicuous in the bright level rays which lit them up and fired the dormer-window of the thatched roof beyond. By and by they dropped into the yard, where amongst the straw they found an egg. They broke and ate it. Then the hen-bird came flying back in great haste to the nest, as if she feared her precious clutch might be chilled and become addled. Later the cock-bird returned to tell her what was happening in the farmyard, and at once flew back to the elder. He was back again in half an hour: indeed he kept flying to and fro until sundown. The hare rejoiced in the restlessness of this arch-mobber of vermin: it gave her a sense of security such as she had not felt since the birth of her young. For her the magpie was an untiring patrol, and further, one gifted with a tongue that would make the boldest fox shrink from the insults it was capable of raining on him. Her fears fled in the presence of this sentinel of the wild, so that for a few minutes during the afternoon she actually fell asleep. "If only there were some night-bird to watch over us," she thought while she sat awaiting dusk. And as soon as darkness fell an owl began hooting. At once, as if she took it for a signal, she stole from the form to attend to her young.

Her visit was most welcome to the jack, who was very sorry when she withdrew. He listened to her retreating steps, and as they died away tried to combat the feeling of loneliness that beset him. In the weary watch that followed he sorely missed the companion of his waking hours. He felt forlorn without her soft, warm side to nestle against; but in a night or two he found something to occupy him. He took to grooming himself, and off and on spent hours brushing his ears and licking his coat, especially the snow-white fur on his belly, which had looked so ghostly as his mother bore him through the dusk. He made himself as clean as a pink, and when the feeling of isolation wore off, as it soon did, he felt as happy as a strong, healthy leveret could feel. Soon, however, his muscles began to ache for want of exercise: they kept urging him to throw aside his fears and break his narrow bounds; but night after night he resisted the impulse. At last inaction became unendurable. Regardless of his mother's monitions and the whispers of instinct, he leapt the rill and raced about the moonlit green like a thing possessed.

Instantly he was joined by his sister, and never perhaps did two leverets enjoy their stolen freedom more. They bounded over each other's back; they leapt the rock by the thorn, clearing it by a good foot; they galloped round and round like performers in a circus. Tiring of this, they rose on their hind legs and sparred with their pads, moving about the fairy ring and patting each other's face like boxers. But whilst they were thus engaged the snapping of a brier disturbed the night and sent them to their seats. With wildly beating hearts they sat till the clumsy badger who had trodden on the spray passed out of hearing; then out they came again and renewed their frolics, which lasted without further interruption till the moon began to pale.

Their mother found them in their seats looking as innocent as could be; but she knew of their escapade from the scent on the green and, recognising in this bid for liberty a token that the time was come for leading them out, she resolved to devote herself to this duty without further delay. So the following night, instead of returning at early dawn, she hurried back in the small hours and surprised the culprits, not, as she expected, in the midst of their games, but nibbling the grass of the green. At the sight of their mother the guilty creatures scurried to their forms, only to bound out at her summons and follow frisking at her heels as she led past the spring to the hill. She breasted the slope at a slow canter, but soon quickened her steps. Half-way up she began doubling, the leverets imitating her twists and turns in a surprising way and with astonishing exactness. Towards daybreak, however, they flagged, and by the time they got back to the green they were so tired that they were content to remain in the form till the hour for exercise came round again.

The hare returned nightly at almost the same moment, and went farther and farther afield as their strength grew, without encountering even in these extended excursions any enemy more formidable than an old badger, who never dreamt of pursuit. It is true that he looked hard at them, but only because of his surprise at seeing survivors of a race which he thought extinct. The instant he satisfied himself they really were hares, he resumed his grunting and crossed the ridge on the way to his earth.

At the first faint blush in the east the hares sped towards the pool that fills the hollow between Bartinney and Chapel Carn Brea. There near the edge of the water the leverets confused their trails and chose their seats. This they did under the eyes of their mother, who watched interestedly from the slope where she lay amongst the heather. As it proved, no precautions were necessary, for no creature came near; indeed, nothing disturbed the drowsy stillness till late in the day, when a breeze sprang up that sent the water in tiny wavelets against the rushy shore. This immunity from molestation was the result of the hare's knowledge of the ways of her enemies, of their retreats, and especially of the times of their coming and going. At every outing they crossed the foul line left by some marauder on its way to the lowland, but—those of the badger excepted—never a homing trail; for the hares were settled in their forms before fox, polecat, and stoat came slinking back to their lairs.

But not even the hare, with cunning quickened by the dependence of her young, could provide against every contingency. On the fourth day of their stay by the pool, when they were back in their seats around the green, they were discovered and attacked by a bloodthirsty little creature that was abroad foraging in the very middle of the morning. The hare's suspicions were first aroused by the angry cries of some small birds in the corner of the nearest field. Soon the demonstration grew more and more distinct, showing that the birds were pursuing the object of their displeasure in the direction of the green. From the first the noise attracted the attention of the magpie. Immediately he saw the birds he cocked his head, now this way now that, as if beholding the most interesting sight of his life. And a strange sight it certainly was; for, accompanied by linnets and finches that fluttered over it, there came with the quick movement of its kind, a weasel, seemingly quite indifferent to the mobbing it received. As soon as it appeared the hare quivered in every limb; but there was no shiver of fear, for when presently the little miscreant scented the jack and stood on its hind legs screaming, to paralyse him with terror, she bounded across the green, and with a stroke of a forepad sent the animal flying into the water. Undaunted, and enraged at this treatment, the weasel now confronted the hare herself, only to be knocked over, trampled on, and spurned to the middle of the green, where it lay on its back kicking as though its last hour was come. Whereupon the magpie, who, considering the weasel too insignificant for his intervention, had hitherto held its tongue, chattered loudly as if to applaud the deed; whilst the hare, whose blood was up, remained within a yard of the weasel, ready to renew the battle should it again show fight. Braver still, the linnet whose eggs the weasel had been sucking, as was evident from the stain on its muzzle, stood within a few inches and upbraided it for the wrong done her, and, frail thing though she was, scarcely deigned to move when shortly it regained its feet and made for the hill. It was not allowed to sneak away unattended; birds and hare—strange allies—accompanied the discomfited little wretch past the spring to the heather, where it wormed its way amongst the stems and hid itself from view. Then the linnets and finches, having avenged their friend, flew back to their thickets; and the hare, crouching low as if frightened now by her own shadow, stole to her form. The magpie still perched on the spray from which he had witnessed the scene. The arch-rogue had thoroughly enjoyed every phase of it, and now that it was over he was all alive, quizzing the spots where the hare and the leverets lay, as if trying to get a view of them amidst the cover. At last he too flew away; then no trace remained of the participators in the drama but a tiny feather that lay where the linnet had stood.

The visit of the weasel had its consequences, for the hare, fearing that the creature would return when she was away foraging, resolved to take the leverets with her at setting-out time, and after she had regained her composure she sat planning the round she would lead them.

---

[1] The doe hare leaves little scent whilst her young are helpless.

CHAPTER II
EDUCATION

The low summons of the hare drew the leverets to her side, and when she set out they followed close at her heels. Late as she was in starting, she picked her way down the rough foothills very slowly and with extreme caution; indeed, so halting was her advance, so mistrustful was she of every rock and bush, that she might have been Fear herself leading her offspring past ambuscades. But the moment she set foot on the reclaimed land—the field where the linnet was roosting by her empty nest—she quickened her steps and passed rapidly from enclosure to enclosure, the novices wondering at the smoothness of the ground and shrinking from the shadows cast by the gates under which they crept.

Soon the little band entered the grassy lane which led past the magpie's elder to the farmhouse, and there the leverets got a scare from some fowls packed as close as they could sit on a limb of the solitary sycamore. The birds mistook the hares for foxes, and in their panic dislodged the rooster from his perch. The extraordinary noise he made, as with a great flapping of wings he fell to the ground, frightened the leverets almost out of their lives; in their terror they pressed so close to their mother's side that the three were for a moment jammed in the gap by which they entered the neighbouring pasture. But the leverets showed no fear of the kine that lay there chewing their cud, or of the ewes and lambs in the next enclosure but one, passing in and out amongst them as unconcernedly as if born and reared in their midst. In the adjoining field the wanderers remained to feed on the abundant crop of clover, which furnished so sumptuous a feast for the leverets after the poor herbage of the green that they would have eaten to excess had not their mother called them off. It was not that, however, which made her lead them away, but her eagerness to show them the country and teach them all she knew. Moreover, she was anxious to acquaint them with their powers, especially with their ability to swim, for it would stand them in good stead when pressed by enemies, as she knew by experience.

So, on leaving the clover, she made in the direction of the moorland pool to which her mother had led her when young, where, owing to the absence of all but the scantiest cover, no enemy could approach unobserved. Annoyed at having to leave the clover, the leverets followed with reluctance, till presently the stillness was broken by the music of running water. At the sound the jack pricked his ears as though he recognised a familiar voice. It was indeed the rill, but swollen now by tributary runnels into a little stream three feet wide at the shallows where the hares crossed. On the bridle-path leading to the hamlet of Crowz-an-Wra the leverets raced up and down, whilst the hare sat on the turfy border by an old cross and watched them. In the profound silence the beating of their pads on the hard surface was loud enough to mask the approach of a stealthy enemy; of this the leverets seemed fully conscious, for they stood motionless at short intervals and listened.

Time after time the only sound that filled the pause was the subdued but solemn roar of the sea about the cliffs of the Land's End. Presently, however, there broke upon it an ominous "patter, patter, patter." In an instant the timorous creatures were flying. Near a heap of stones they stopped and listened with ears a-cock, and there again came that "patter, patter, patter," very faint at first but rapidly growing more and more distinct. Whoever the pursuer, he was coming along at a rapid pace. The rhythm of the footfall fascinated the hares. They stood with eyes fixed on the track to get a view the moment the creature showed. But all at once the noise ceased, to the obvious disquiet of the hare. She snuffled and snorted as when in the presence of the weasel, and set off again at a swinging pace with the leverets, now thoroughly alarmed, obedient to her every movement. Suddenly she bounded from the path to the selvedge of turf. On landing she leapt again and again. The leverets followed as if tied to her, leaping nearly as far as she did, for already they could cover nine feet in a spring. Then they sped over croft and field till, quite a mile from the track, they came to a level waste with the pool in its midst. She was about to lead them into the water when she noticed the jack on his hind legs surveying the moor. Stung by this reminder of her negligence, she leapt to the bank and looked in the direction of the trail. She looked long, but saw no sign of the pursuer, and then, completely satisfied that all was well, rejoined the leverets, who followed her without shrinking towards the middle of the pool.

It seemed as if the long-legged creatures would never get out of their depth, yet they lost their foothold at last, fell to swimming, and soon gained the opposite bank. In their wet coats they looked more leggy than ever, but regained their usual appearance after shaking themselves a time or two. Then the hare again scanned the almost bare surface and, seeing nothing, gave up all thought of the enemy and devoted herself to her young. Her eyes were all for them: she had not another glance for her back trail.

Her lack of vigilance was the opportunity of the dog fox who had struck their line in the clover-field and followed it to the moor, which he was now scrutinising from the only rock that rose above it. He looked everywhere but at the right spot. In his ignorance of a hare's ways he did not examine the pool, till a slight disturbance of the surface arrested his wandering gaze: even then he thought that the ripples were caused by wildfowl; but the moon emerged from the black cloud that had obscured it, and revealed the three hares frisking in the shallows.

The fox licked his chops at the rare sight, and hopeless though he thought the stalk, resolved to attempt it. Instantly he slipped from the rock and stole forward, taking advantage of the meanest tuft to conceal his approach. Yet for all his cleverness he was a conspicuous object, and had the hare been alert she could not have failed to see him. Once, indeed, she did seem uneasy, as if vaguely conscious of danger; the fox, whose eyes never left her, was quick to see that, and when she looked his way he was rigid in his stride and escaped observation. But immediately she turned he resumed his advance, and soon it seemed he might succeed in his murderous design. Noiseless as a phantom, he drew nearer and nearer till, with ears flat and body crouching to the ground, he reached the stunted rushes on the margin of the pool.

Now he was so near the hares that when they shook themselves the spray all but reached him. Again and again with his cruel eyes he measured the distance, and as often refrained from launching himself: he would not spoil the stalk by a rash step, for at any moment the hares might approach within reach of his spring, or they might re-enter the pool and be at his mercy. And it looked as if his patience would be rewarded, for in a second or two, seconds which seemed hours, the jack moved towards him. Another yard and his fate would be sealed. But he stopped to scratch one of his ears; and when he was about to advance again there came from out the stillness a breath of wind laden with the foul scent of the marauder. Quicker than thought the affrighted creature whipped round and followed his mother and sister, who were already in full retreat. As the leveret turned, the fox made a tremendous spring, but he landed four feet short and could only make a frantic effort to overtake it. For a score yards or so the chase was most exciting, neither gained nor lost; but the terrific pace was beyond the power of the fox to maintain, and as he fell behind the jack drew farther and farther away, increasing his lead so much that presently reynard desisted from pursuit. Panting he stood and watched, craning his neck to get a last view as the conspicuous scuts disappeared from sight. Then, after a glance at the sky, the disappointed hunter made back over the moor, slowly at first but quickening his pace as he went, his neat footprints commingling here and there in the soft ground with the nail-pricks of the hares.

The hares, on discovering that the fox had given up pursuit, slackened speed, and when they reached Brea Farm lingered awhile to feed before withdrawing for the day. In the grey dawn they crossed the wall and made their way towards the old chantry. Half-way to the summit the leverets, apparently without a hint, separated first from the hare and then from each other, and secreted themselves in seats where the sun would find them early and where, weary after their long round, they soon passed from drowsiness into a sound sleep.

The week that followed was singularly void of disquieting incidents; nevertheless it was a period of great importance in the life of the jack, because of the signs of independence that manifested themselves in his conduct. Hitherto he had been tractable enough considering his sex; under the influence of fear he had been a model of good behaviour; now all was changed, suddenly changed. The night following his escape from the fox, he stayed behind in the clover-field long after his mother had gone on, and—a thing he had never done before—took no notice of her repeated calls except to twitch his ears as if annoyed at her persistency. Then the very next night he obstinately refused to leave the wheatfield, though his mother shook with fright as she told him that she had just seen a polecat looking out of a rabbit-hole in the hedge, and that to stay might cost him his life. But she might as well have besought the granite rubbing-post near them for all the heed the self-willed creature gave; he simply went on nibbling. On both occasions she had to come back and fetch him, and thoroughly did he deserve the drumming he got.

He disliked being punished, but did not mend his ways. Indeed he grew worse. A few nights later—it was Tuesday, because the Sennen men were at bell-practice—his mother all at once missed him and, going back, found him standing on his hind legs gazing at a scarecrow. The beaver-hatted object had excited his curiosity, and he was waiting to see it move. That was no great offence: before two hours had passed, however, the incorrigible fellow gave her the slip, and by making use of the "leaping" ruse she had taught him, prevented her from tracing him. She gave him up for lost; but the truant was happy enough, roaming amidst the barley or playing among the shadows cast by a stone-circle, confident in his knowledge of the country and his ability to find his way back to the hill. Yet he must have had misgivings or got scared, for he returned to the Carn at a very early hour; and there his mother found him looking sheepish enough after his spell of freedom. She had not sought him in order to rebuke him, for she had given up both complaining and correction; she had come solely to satisfy herself that he was safe. In a way she rejoiced in his independence, knowing that the time was fast approaching when he would have to fend for himself.

[*To face p. 32.*

AUTHOR'S SKETCH-MAP OF THE SCENE OF THE STORY.

And because the moment of separation was imminent, she led him and his sister that very night to the spot beloved above all others by the hares of the Land's End, the dunes of Sennen and the long strand of Whitesand Bay. She took a bee-line from the Carn and, leading at a good pace, soon reached her destination, where the leverets, pleased by the feel of the sand under their pads, hopped and skipped like lambs, or like runners in an arena with dunes for spectators and waves to applaud, galloped after their fleet-footed mother with the speed of the wind. Their disappearance into the gloom and sudden reappearance made them seem quite uncanny on that uncanny foreshore, haunted, if tradition be true, by drowned sailors who hail one another across the beach. The surge beat on the shore, the swell boomed in the near caves, the breeze stirred the rushes tufting the dunes: except for these the hares were alone; but the light gleamed across the waters from the Longships, and near midnight the faint sweep of muffled oars told where the Preventive Patrol crossed the bay. The unusual noise caused the hares to cease their scamperings and look seaward. Yet danger was not there but at the foot of the dunes, where a half-wild cat crouched near the path by which they came and eagerly awaited their return. All unconscious of her presence the hares left the beach to play on the rocks at Genvor Head, now uncovered by the tide; there the jack, prompted by the adventurous spirit that was ever urging him to do "something grand," made along the ledge towards the point over which the sea was dashing dangerously. Luckily his mother observed him and drove him back, despite the efforts he made to get past her. So he turned sulky and lagged behind her and his sister when presently they crossed the dunes for the feeding-ground. The cat, who had been a close observer of the scene on the rocks, and was not a little chagrined when two of the hares passed wide of her station, now fixed her attention on the jack, as his slow movements made her think he was wounded and might fall an easy prey. But again she was doomed to disappointment; for while she debated whether to rush at the leveret or stay where she was, the jack recovered his temper and went off at full speed over the dunes.

Graymalkin naturally thought she had seen the last of him. Leaving her hiding-place, she went and sat by the mouth of a rabbit-hole, to try to secure one of the occupants when it came out. She might have been there a quarter of an hour when to her surprise she saw the jack pass on his way to the beach. He was making straight for the rocks. Without a moment's hesitation she followed, so quickly that when he reached the point of the rocks, she had gained the shore end and cut off his retreat. Yellow though she was, it is a wonder that he did not see her as she crossed the sand, but he did not; what first drew his attention was the mewing noise she made whilst creeping panther-like to the spot where the rocks contract to a narrow waist which the hare must pass. There she stopped. At sight of the hideous creature he realised the straits he was in, and in his terror backed involuntarily nearer and nearer to the edge; the sea as it surged over the rock reached half-way up his legs, the spray drenched him, but he seemed indifferent to it all. He looked thoroughly woebegone; he was surely doomed; if the sea did not get him, the cat would. Presently he stopped backing when only six inches from the edge and, pulling himself together, tried to think of a way of escape. But he found it difficult to think under the eyes of the brute crouching there. His best chance was to swim to Genvor Beach, but this never entered his head; the bewildered fellow was debating as best he could whether it was better to spring over the cat or dodge her. Had it not been for the bunch of seaweed at the very spot on which he would alight he would have tried the spring; but in the circumstances he decided to risk all on the zigzag ruse, at which he was an adept, having played it with his sister on the green. Like an arrow from a bow he shot forward as if he meant to pass to the right of the cat; as soon as his pads touched the rock, like lightning he swerved to the left; then he shot ahead again and so got away without a scratch. The cat, thoroughly outwitted, had sprung for the place where she had supposed the hare would be; but she sprang at the air and fell into the sea. Almost immediately a wave washed her on the rocks, and there she stood silent while, with eyes like living coals, she watched the jack disappear over the dunes.

The terrified fellow ran for two miles along his mother's trail without halting; then coming to some briers he stopped to nibble the shoots, for he was very hungry. He would have stayed longer than he did had not the rosy foreglow in the sky warned him to be off. So again he took to the trail and hurried along at his best pace, scaring the boy at Brea Farm, who took him for a pixie, as he whisked past the gap on his way to the Fairies' Green, where for an hour or more his mother and sister had been sitting in their forms. The magpies saw him coming, but chattered no reproach to the belated creature; though to a fox cub they would have shown no mercy. After he had made his toilet, enjoying the taste of the salt water, he sat moving his jaws as if he were chewing the cud. He was really crushing some grains of sand, of which he had picked up a mouthful on the beach, and the curious noise completely puzzled the magpies, who tried in vain to locate it. The dew was being fast dried up by the sun before it ceased: then the slow regular rise and fall of his flank told he was asleep.

That night the hare took the jack and his sister a way they had not been before. It led over Caer Bran to Boswarthen, where all three gambolled like mad things in the corn before going down the hill to Tregonebris. There, after feasting on the pinks in which the farmer's wife took special pride, they passed to the field of mowing-grass before the house and played on the heap of earth in the far corner, the hare joining in the frolics with a zest she had not shown since she led them up Bartinney. By this time the air, which had been oppressively close, had become more sultry than ever, till towards midnight the impending storm broke, zigzagging the inky sky with fierce lightning. Immediately the silence was rent by claps of thunder, and a torrent of rain followed which drenched the hares before they could gain the shelter of the hedge. When at length it ceased they galloped up and down the path leading to the house and dried themselves; but they were drenched again before dawn. They looked a forlorn little band as they ambled over the fields in a downpour. Yet, miserable though their plight seemed, they passed a clump of brambles which at least offered a partial refuge; farther up the hill they passed another, more inviting still; indeed they kept on as if regardless of all cover till they reached the summit of Caer Bran, where they sought seats under the furze mantling the slope of the outer of the earthworks that crown it. The wind blew, the rain pelted, but the high bank and domed roof protected them from all discomfort save that caused by the drippings of the sodden bushes. This the creatures endured through the long day without once stirring in their forms.

The hare rose at her usual time, but instead of setting out forthwith as was her custom she went to where the jack lay and licked his face again and again, which she had not done since he was weaned. What was the meaning of this extraordinary display of affection? Was it to solace him for the severity of her schooling and growing coldness? Not at all. It was to mark the moment of separation; it was her last office to him; it was her farewell greeting. The jack understood; his behaviour showed it. For when presently his mother and sister set out, he, hitherto always the second afoot, remained in the form and watched them pass from sight. As the bushes hid them, he was on the point of rising to follow, but restrained himself and sat listening as if in expectation of the call. The low bleat for which he hearkened did not come; there was no sound but the moan of the wind about the old earthworks. Then the seriousness of the position came home to him: his mother and sister had gone out of his life; the freedom for which he had been yearning was at last his. Was he elated? Far from it. A sense of forlornness possessed him, but this was soon to be banished by the high spirits that surged through him and thrilled his whole being. Whilst he sat addressing himself to the struggle before him the sky suddenly cleared, and where all had been black, stars shone in the steadfast blue.

Then he arose, stretched his perfect limbs, and, after a glance along the trail, set his face for the farm-lands to which his mother had the previous night introduced him.

CHAPTER III
INDEPENDENCE

The leveret's wonderful memory for country he had once been over enabled him to find his way straight back to the farm, where with timid steps he passed from enclosure to enclosure, exploring his domain. In his round he came on a field of clover, another of turnips, two of corn, pastures with sheep and cattle, and a pound with a donkey in it, familiar objects which served to make him forget his solitary condition till he came to the scene of the previous night's frolics; then the thought of his mother and sister flashed across his mind: he became alive to his loneliness. But a voice within whispered, "Courage, courage, all will soon be well"; at this he took heart and strove to forget the past as he resumed his way, observant of everything and alert to the many dangers of the night.

In a field of mowing-grass and again in the oats he caught the rank scent of an enemy—luckily in time to avoid it and withdraw without being discovered. Now and again he stopped to nibble a bit of tempting herbage; but he did not settle down to feed until the small hours, when he returned to the clover. Here he remained till the first flush in the sky warned him he must seek a retreat in which to pass the day. Twice he made towards the gate as if he were leaving the field, as often retraced his steps, presently repaired to the spot where the clover was most luxuriant, and lay there. No sooner, however, had he sat down than he realised that the stems which shut out the sight of everything prevented him from seeing an enemy, should one approach. The lack of outlook troubled him: soon he imagined that he could hear the faint sound of a stealthy footfall. To satisfy himself that he was mistaken he kept raising his head and looking round until, unable to endure the misery any longer, he stole from the seat and hurried back to the highest part of the farm, where a hedge had taken his fancy as he had crossed from the barley to the oats.

There, amongst the coarse grasses, beneath the fronds of a solitary brake-fern, he sat with his face to the dawn-wind, which played with his whiskers, swayed the ears of the barley, and buffeted the smoke rising from the chimney of the homestead. The light was still grey, but beyond the low roof of the byre the hills stood expectant of the sun, whose fiery disc soon bathed summit and slope with its richest rays. The conspicuous heights attracted the eyes of the leveret till the orb rose higher and made a glory of the dew on the leaves of the tree amidst the barley; then the sparkling beads won and held his gaze; later the tree itself so absorbed his attention that he seemed to be wondering what it did there. It certainly was a strange place for a tree, especially for a fruit-tree, though it was not strange to the people familiar with its story. The field, or rather a part of it, had formerly been a garden—it is still called Johanna's Garden; and sentiment had caused the tree to be spared, though it interfered with the plough and attracted badgers who trod down the crop.

The leveret had not been long in his form before one of these animals crossed the opposite bank, shaking the dew from the wild roses that festooned the creep, and made its way through the barley and the oats to the sett at the foot of the steep slope. Here a colony of badgers lived. The lane in the corn was their highway, and the tree a convenient stretching-post, so that next to the crowing of the cocks, the scratching noise made by powerful claws was the most familiar noise of the grey dawn. Luckily the leveret had no fear of the badgers, no more fear of them indeed than of the long-tailed tit whom he watched coming and going with food for a brood of insatiable nestlings in the near furze-bush. The cries of the young tits, all eager for the food she brought, were at times the only sound that broke the silence of the sequestered spot; there were days when scarcely a breath stirred, when the stalks of the barley were as motionless as the stem of the tree, and the shadow of the frond looked like a stain on the leveret's coat.

He enjoyed the slumbrous peace, and revelled in the noonday heat that shimmered above the array of barley ears and veiled with a pearly haze valley and hills and all the land between. It was a delightful time, which in his innocence he thought would last for ever. He knew nothing of the ways of husbandry, of the harvesting of crops by the dwellers of the homestead, whence by day came shout and song, and where the strange light glowed in the early hours of foraging time. He did not know that man was lord of the earth; as little did he realise that he himself was man's guest. His own view was quite different. He thought that the clover, the corn, and the pinks grew for him, that fern and heather flourished to afford him cover, that hedge and hill rose above the level merely to furnish him with outlook. He even thought that the sun rose to warm him, that moon and stars shone to light his steps; and he found the world a most delectable place, despite the number of his enemies.

A somewhat rude awakening befell him on the thirteenth day of his independence, when the field was invaded by the farm folk. Their coming, or rather their inrush, had nothing to do with the harvesting of the barley, which was yet green; they were drawn thither by an incident of farm life that is attended with as much noise as human beings are capable of making. The hubbub broke out near the house some two furlongs away. Even at that distance the din was disquieting, but it grew louder and louder and caused the leveret more and more perturbation. Whilst he wondered what it all meant, a swarm of bees came flying over the hedge and settled on the tree. In less than a minute three boys, two men, and a woman came tumbling pell-mell over the hedge, shouting "Brownie, Brownie," and beating frying-pans and milk-pails. The boy who led soon espied the cluster of bees hanging to the branch, and cried, "Here they are, faither, fastened on the old medlar-tree."

"Th—that's lucky, lad," replied the father breathlessly as his face showed above the hedge, "I feared we'd seed the laist of 'em. Go and fetch a skep and my hat, and don't forget the bellows, for I've hardly a brith left in me. But, dang me," he added angrily, on sighting the lane in the barley, "what a mess they badgers have made of the corn. It's all through that theer tree, and down it shall come."

"What, Johanna's tree? Cut down Johanna's tree? You'll do nawthin' of the kind, maister. 'Twas her pride, good soul, so I've heered granny say. Cut it down? Why, 'twould be enough to make her turn in her grave, and perhaps visit 'ee, who do knaw? And only think a minit, you'd have lost that swarm of bees, and a handsome swarm it is. Iss fay, and worth a bra bit; 'a swarm of bees in June is worth a silver spoon,' and you'd have lost it if the tree hadn't been theere."

"Well, well, Betty, most likely you're right. I never looked at it that way."

"Ah, maister, it don't take much to make people forget their obligations."

"Now, now, Betty, have done, theere's a good woman; I spoke in haste. I'll never lay hands on Johanna's tree. And here comes our Jesse already. The lad's as fast as a hare, and if he's forgotten the bellows he's remembered the cloth to ground the hive on."

Taking the skep, the farmer shook the bees into it and laid it on the cloth which Jesse had spread at the foot of the tree. "They'll do all right theere till the sun is gone, when I'll come myself and fetch 'em. Now let's make haste back and finish our fish and taties, or they'll be too cold to be worth eating. What do you say, Dick?"

"You're right, maister, a cold pilcher ed'n much account, nor a cold tatie nother. I'd as soon sit down to a basin of sky blue and sinker,[2] and that ed'n sayin' much." With that, man and master, Betty and the boys quitted the field, leaving the hare to his reflections.

The whole proceeding was a mystery to the timid wildling, who had kept to his seat notwithstanding Betty's shrill voice and gesticulations. Some hares would have slipped away, but it was instinctive in him to lie close until found; a trait of his strain which went far to explain the survival of his forbears amidst the gradual disappearance of their kind. But though satisfied that he was not the object of the visit as he had at first feared, he was glad when the party went away and left him to solitude. The rest of the day was without incident, save that the farmer, true to his word, came and fetched the bees at sundown.

The swarming of the bees and their capture was followed a week later by a further disquieting incident, the cutting of the clover. It quite took his breath away one morning when he reached the gate, to find the crop levelled and the look of the enclosure changed almost beyond recognition: the hedges too had grown so much taller. The timid fellow shrank from entering the field; indeed the presence of three rabbits feeding there would alone have sufficed to prevent it. On several occasions these very rabbits had shown themselves hostile and driven him off. Rabbits were by no means plentiful on his beats; he had not seen more than a score; and as for hares, he had not only not met with one, he had not crossed a single trail. He was the solitary survivor of his kind, with enemies on every hand. Nevertheless, confident in the protection which his wiles and speed afforded him, he enjoyed life to the full, roaming over the farms in the highest of spirits.

But though he exulted in his powers he ran no risks; even the buck his father had not been so wary as he. Whilst feeding he kept to the middle of the field, where at frequent intervals he sat up and looked about him, first to leeward, then to windward, his nostrils working all the time, to assure himself that no enemy was near. Then he always slowed down when approaching a gate or creep, in order to learn by sight or smell whether a fox or one of the farm cats was lying in wait for him; once he winded a fox and withdrew noiselessly as a shadow, leaving the fox none the wiser. He was quick in distinguishing marauders by their footfall and by the rustling they made in threading the ripe corn.

With the arrival of harvest, however, he was completely puzzled by the loud outcry that arose on the farm-lands. It was always the same, and caused by the reapers hailing the cutting of the last sheaf.[3] Sometimes while he was in the form, sometimes when he was afoot, the silence would be broken by a voice proclaiming aloud, "I haben, I haben," followed by many voices asking, "What have 'ee? What have 'ee?" and the instant response, "A neck, a neck," welcomed by loud hurrahs. Save for these acclamations of farmer and farm-hands, he was wise in the lore of the countryside; and with knowledge came confidence, which led to his wandering farther and farther afield. He roamed as far as three miles from the seat, to which he nevertheless continued to return, until he happened on a wild bottom which the country folk have named Golden Valley.

It was a beautiful starlight night when he came to the brow overlooking it, and sat down to gaze at the mill, the pool above it, and the glimpses of stream showing in the gorse like silver stitched on black velvet. A will o' the wisp was flitting to and fro near the bend of the valley, and a white owl was searching the stubble before the miller's cottage; otherwise nothing stirred; so presently the leveret made his way down and down the rugged hillside to the stream. This he followed as far as the mill-pool; then, after glancing round the rushy margin, he retraced his steps and crossed the stream below the mill. Sometimes along the bank, sometimes within a stone's throw as the bushes allowed, he held on to the swampy ground where the weird light still floated hither and thither and, passing between patches of iris and watermint, came to some mounds carpeted with thyme, on which he remained to feed. From there he overlooked a sheet of water, half-circled with alders, a fowler's hut peeping from beneath a cluster of them. No bird rested on the water, which was marked only by the rings made by trout rising at the white moths that came within their reach. It was a very peaceful scene, with no breath of wind to diffuse the scent given out by meadow-sweet and camomile.

The hungry fellow nibbled unceasingly at the aromatic herb, avoiding the glow-worms which dotted the mounds. On the furze they were even more numerous, so that their golden-green lamps lit up the beads of dew on the spiders' webs. But the leveret rarely interrupted his feast to look about him; only once did he scratch his ears, and whilst so engaged had his attention attracted by a shrill whistle from the stream below the pool. Turning his head, he saw an otter and two cubs come over the bank which dammed the pool, and enter the water with so little disturbance as to make them seem uncanny. When they dived, their progress would have been most difficult to follow had it not been for the leaping of the trout, for the waves they raised were hardly noticeable even where the water was shallowest. The otters rose at different parts of the pool, each with a trout in its mouth, swam to the bank, and there lay at full length to devour their take. After fishing for nearly half an hour the animals fell to playing, now in the water, now on the bank, at times even in the open spaces among the bushes. From one of these the cubs espied the leveret. At once ceasing their gambols, they watched him nibble the herbage, their nostrils working all the time. The leveret, who showed no fear of the strange, short-legged creatures, was still feeding when the otter recalled her cubs and led them up the stream, but he was nearly satisfied, and shortly made his way along the dam and up the opposite hill to the downs, over which he kept wandering and wandering as if in search of a seat. Yet this was not his object. He had already made up his mind where he would pass the coming day, took the hint from a homing badger that it was time to be ensconced, returned to the valley, and hid amongst the rushes bordering the mill-pool, at a spot almost midway between the inflow and the hatch.

He had hardly settled down when the otter and her cubs hurried by along the opposite bank, on their way to a reedy marsh a mile above. Then all was quiet till, at peep of day, a kingfisher came and fished from a branch of the alder overhanging the inflow; the tinkle of the water as she struck it made a pretty sound in the silent dawn. Later, just as the smoke rose from the miller's chimney, a moorhen led out her brood as if to teach them the geography of the pool, for she kept taking them from creeklet to creeklet till the miller came to raise the hatch and drove them all away. The hum of the water-wheel brought back to the leveret's memory the swarm of bees and the unforgettable din of the reapers; but if he looked for the invasion of his new quarters by a posse of men and boys he must have been agreeably disappointed when, early in the forenoon, there came only a solitary angler, whose entry was so noiseless as scarcely to disturb the peace of the quiet spot. Indeed the newcomer stood for a second or two surveying the pool from the opening between the withies before the leveret was aware of his presence. On the discovery the timid creature thought, naturally enough, that the pair of restless black eyes were scanning the bank in search of him; he did not know they were drawn now here, now there, by the rising trout. The angler was a tall, spare man of aquiline features, attired in grey tweed suit and wearing a dove-coloured top-hat, about which some fly-casts were neatly wound. His upright figure, thick black curly hair, in which the few grey hairs seemed out of place, above all the comeliness of face, marked him as a man between thirty and forty years of age. So one would have judged as he stood, though the ease with which he leapt the ditch to the sedges spoke rather of twenty-five.

He took his position on the turfy bank over against the leveret, and at once began whipping together the three pieces of the rod he had removed from the cloth case, working with extreme haste as if he feared that the fish would cease to rise before he was ready. When the joints were securely tied, he fixed the reel, ran the line through the rings, and attached the cast with coch-y-bondhu for end fly, and red palmer for dropper. Surely he is too impatient to soak the gut before casting; no, he flings it into the little creek at his side and, to kill the time of waiting, paces nervously up and down the bank. After four turns he took up the rod and began casting, the flies falling lightly on the rippled surface. At the third throw he was fast in a fish, but just failed to steer it clear of a bed of weeds for which it made, and consequently lost it. At the very next cast, when the flies fell close to the hatch, he rose and hooked a bigger fish. This leapt out of the water and broke its hold. He was much vexed, as the suddenly compressed lips showed, but as he was about to give vent to his feelings a still larger fish rose under the bank, close to the leveret. This sight checked the word on the very tip of his tongue. The cast, a long one even from the edge of the bank to which he now moved up, was rendered difficult if not impossible by the withies, which twice caught the tail-fly at the beginning of the forward cast and as often caused the Squire to give utterance to a monosyllable delivered with staccato sharpness. At length he succeeded in clearing the withies and getting the line out to its full length. It was a good, clean cast, and would have been perfect had the pool been a yard wider; as it was, the coch-y-bondhu caught in the rushes and, despite the coaxing treatment to which the Squire subjected it, refused to come away, the only result being to alarm the hare and raise the ire of the angler. Worse was to come; for presently the trout, which kept rising with irritating persistence, seized the dropper, hooked itself, and in the violent struggle that followed broke the tackle and got away with the red palmer in its jaw.

The situation was beyond the power of words, and it was strange to see how the Squire met it. He dashed the rod to the ground, he paced up and down the bank like a man demented, he shook his fist at the withies, he shook it at the rushes, and kept shaking it till at length, after having beaten a path on the turf, he had worked off his rage. Then he sat down on the bank, filled his pipe and blew clouds of smoke. The tobacco had a soothing effect: soon he was debating with himself whether to break the cast or go and release the hook. He resolved to go round, but first he would try to free it where he sat. So he took up the rod, flicked the line, and then, as bad luck would have it, the fly came away. Yes, it was bad luck, for few things would have surprised and delighted the Squire more than the sight of a hare, whom he must have disturbed had he been compelled to go round. He would have been thrilled by the discovery that the hare was not, as he believed, extinct on his land. But it was a joy postponed; he was to see the hare before the year was out, in circumstances as different from those as imagination can conceive.

And meanwhile the hare, whose immunity from molestation had been remarkable, was destined to undergo a series of terrible trials, the first of which, strangely enough, befell it that very night.

---

[2] Barley-bread and skimmed milk.

[3] The old harvest custom of "crying the neck."

CHAPTER IV
CHASED BY POLECATS

The sun had sunk below the hill, and Golden Valley lay in shadow and repose. Zekiah, the miller, his work done at last, sat smoking his pipe on the bench by the door; the mill-wheel was at rest, and the stream was slowly refilling the nearly emptied pond where, from time to time, a wave in the shallows betrayed the movement of a trout. Overhead a few swifts yet wheeled: but yellow-hammer, whinchat, blackcap, whitethroat, and long-tailed tit had sought roosting-places in the furze, and the magpie that haunted the mill had withdrawn to his perch in the hawthorn. For them the hour for rest had come; the moment when nocturnal creatures quit their retreat drew near. The bat was on the point of leaving the crevice under the eaves; the owl in the ivied scarp, the vixen in the earth overlooking the fowling-pool watched the shadows deepen, and still more impatient was the leveret, who already after a two nights' absence was longing for a feast of clover. With the peeping of the stars he sprang from the form, leapt the stream at the inflow, and gaining the crest of the hill, made over the upland almost straight as a crow flies for his destination.

He was in the highest of spirits; the nearer he came to the field the more determined he was to show fight to the rabbits should they combine to drive him from it. The thought never entered his head that any other creatures would intervene between him and his feast, much less that before he could reach the feeding-ground he would be turned into a terror-stricken fugitive; yet so it proved.

On, on he sped until he reached the pasture adjoining the clover; he was within a stone's throw of the gate when he heard the patter of feet on the other side of the hedge; his curiosity was aroused, and he stood still to see the creatures pass the gap a dozen yards to his rear. He expected to view a troop of rats, of which he had met many in the standing corn; to his horror it proved to be a family of polecats, moving so slowly in single file that, though there were only six in all, he thought the procession would never come to an end. All peered through the gap; the last actually stopped and scrutinised the leveret, but concluding that he was one of the many stones that littered the ground, galloped off after the others. It was a narrow escape, for had the leveret raised head or ears he must have been recognised and have drawn the bloodthirsty crew upon him.

The sight of the polecats had so frightened him that he was incapable of movement; it was some minutes before he had sufficiently recovered to continue on his way. Near the gate he stopped and looked back, and once more after entering the field, but without seeing a sign of the enemy. Then he cast his eyes vaguely over the field, the goal of his longing. Not a rabbit was to be seen; the patch of uncut clover looked most tempting. Did he hasten to nibble the succulent leaves? Not at all: he never went near them; he moved away, urged by the impulse to put as great a distance as possible between himself and the polecats, for he felt sure they would follow his trail. All at once he broke into a panic-stricken flight, and kept it up as far as the barley-field, which had been cut in his absence. On the hedge by the tit's deserted nest he stood and listened with ears erect. He expected to hear the whimpering chorus that he had once heard in the valley below, the cry that would confirm his fears. But there was no sound, not even a slight rustling of the medlar leaves. The silence, however, brought him no comfort. It could not dispel the dread which kept him wandering aimlessly about the oatfield like a thing awaiting its doom; so that he must have wasted half an hour before leaving by the gate at the lower corner and galloping across the long meadow where some bullocks glared at him as he sped past. In the small enclosure beyond he stopped to nibble one of the turnips growing there, but so nervous was he that the pigeon drinking at the woodland pool does not raise its head more often than he. His eyes are directed to the spot on the hedge where he had passed; for he is sure that the polecats before now have struck his trail.

His apprehension proved correct. The polecats had happened on his line amongst the furze above the mill-pool, and run it in the right direction from the first. More than once the mother, conscious of the wide circuit made by a hare, was on the point of abandoning the trail; but the sight of her kittens revelling in the scent got the better of her judgment and induced her to keep on. She led her young at the utmost speed they were capable of maintaining, arresting her steps only to scan each field she came to, in the hope of seeing and being seen by the hare, who she knew would be paralysed at the sight of her. She never dreamt that the hare had already seen her and was under the spell of her influence; though the knowledge could not have hastened the pursuit, inasmuch as the kittens were hurrying on as fast as their legs could carry them.

The distance that separated the hunters from the quarry was not great. When they entered the clover the leveret was only just leaving the oats; when they were crossing the barley stubble he was still nibbling the turnips; but he gained after that. For while the polecats were busy working out the tortuous line in the oats he forged ahead and gained High Down, where he busied himself in laying a most intricate maze. He moved hither and thither criss-crossing the trail incessantly, knowing that his life depended on its intricacy. It was well that he was thoroughly absorbed in his task, for had he stopped and listened he could hardly have failed to hear the shrill cry of his pursuers as they bounded across the long meadow. On gaining the hedge-top they stood scrutinising the rows of turnips as if they expected to see the game there; and very odd they looked standing side by side on their hind legs, their eyes shining like glow-worms. But the quarry was nowhere to be seen, so presently mother and kittens leapt to the ground and resumed the full cry, which they kept up over the undulating field beyond, round the edge of the swamp, and below the pair of haggard thorns between which the pack passed.

Meanwhile the leveret, his task well done, was on the point of leaving the downs. He was perhaps a score yards from the gate when the cry he had been so long expecting fell on his ears and rendered him all but helpless. Some hares would have lain down and awaited their fate; others would have squealed and hastened it; but the leveret's courage was high, and, stifling the cry which sought for utterance, he battled as best he could against the paralysing weakness that assailed him, and dragged himself yard by yard towards the gate. Suddenly the cry ceased: the polecats had come on the maze, and in silence devoted themselves to the business of unravelling it. With the cessation of the blood-curdling chorus the leveret's power gradually returned; he drew farther and farther away, seemingly all uncertain as to his goal. At one moment he headed for the form on the hedge; at another for the mound where he had sat once or twice when the wind was northerly; but in the end he set his face for the form by the pool, and to this direction he kept. The polecats, maddened by the delay, had been displaying a feverish energy in their attempt to discover the true line. Each worked independently of the other, and not a kitten looked to the mother for guidance. Theirs was indeed a difficult task: no pack of harriers would have accomplished it without aid of man; yet the wildlings, with a persistence that would not be denied, after two hours' search succeeded in recovering the line by which the leveret had left the field.

Strangely enough the discovery was made by the smallest of the litter, who, after raising the cry of "found," sat on his haunches and gazed about him, as if he expected to view the game. He continued to sit even after his mother had taken up the trail, but presently fell into his place at the end of the long file and joined in the full-tongued chorus. Increased speed now marked the pursuit. The pack was running for blood, and running as they knew against time, for night was yielding to the grey dawn. Already the cocks were crowing, and soon a farm boy was heard calling the cows. At other times the polecats would have stopped, perhaps slunk away to cover; now they gave no heed, no more indeed than to the ruddy sky that told of the coming sun. True that, save for the occasional cry of a kitten, they had ceased their whimperings; otherwise they behaved as if it were the dead of night, going from corner to corner of even the biggest fields, and when at last they came to the mill-lane, following it with a daring that wild creatures rarely display.

The miller's wife caught sight of the polecat as it leapt from the wall, and then watched the spring of kitten after kitten till she was almost tongue-tied with amazement. At last she screamed out: "Zekiah, Zekiah, there's a passel of fitchers under the window; they're running something, I'm sure they are. Wust 'ee, jump out and mob them, thee lie-abed, they'll take no notice of a woman." Whereupon the miller sprang out of bed, thrust his head through the open window, and shouted: "Ah, you bold, imprent varmints, ah! . . . you stinking old night-trade. Be off wi' 'ee. Ah! ah! ah!"

Heedless of the rating, the pack made for the bank of the pool and found another maze awaiting them there. This discouraged the kittens, as their movements showed. But their mother knew that this maze was the hare's last ruse, that he was squatting near; and surely she must have communicated this knowledge to her young, or why should they have suddenly thrown off their lethargy and displayed the almost fiendish activity they did? In an instant the bank was alive with their undulating forms. They darted in and out amongst the sedge; they swam the ditch and twisted about amongst the stems of the withies; again and again they gathered at the spot where the Squire had first stood to fish; for from there the leveret, by a long leap, had gained the pool and swum to the opposite bank. It was the sheet of water that had decided him to make for the form amidst the rushes, and there he was sitting, motionless and helpless.

Luckily he could see nothing of the black, restless creatures, not even their arched backs or raised heads; but the smell of their rank bodies polluted the air, so he knew they were there defiling with their presence the sweet tranquillity of the scene. The absence of all trace of scent near the water, however, baffled the polecats. They could not trace the hare beyond the take-off place, and the clouded water where he had stirred the mud in the shallows contained no message for them.

The growing light was beginning to cause uneasiness to the band; nevertheless one of them proceeded to draw the farther bank; it was the tiny fellow who had recovered the line on High Down. Twice he approached the edge of the pool as if he intended to swim to the other side, but withdrew, made along the bank, crossed at the inflow and at once began questing amongst the rushes. Nearer and nearer he came to the helpless prey, was indeed close on it when the magpie, returning to the thorn by the withies, espied him and forthwith set up the most irritating and persistent chatter. The polecat was greatly disconcerted by the mobbing of the bird, and presently, unable to endure the insults longer, leapt at it where it fluttered just beyond his reach. Maddened by failure he kept on springing at the black-and-white pest till he came to the hatch, up which he climbed to the cross-piece and, careless of both hare and bird, sat there listening to the miller, who was now abroad.

The footfall of the miller and the noise he made in pulling the faggots out of the furze-rick caused the polecat little disquietude; but the moment Zekiah began whistling "Pop goes the Weasel," he leapt to the sward and bounded after his mother, already in full retreat with the rest of the litter, towards a deserted quarry where she had decided to pass the rest of the day.

CHAPTER V
A DELUSIVE REFUGE

The night after that terrible chase the hare made his way back to the farm; but there he met only fresh troubles. First he was driven from Johanna's Garden by a man cutting the hedge, and compelled to slink away in a blaze of sunshine, which was torture to him; next, when sitting in the clover he was pestered by a yearling, that kept rubbing him with her nose. Despite the buffeting he gave her, she annoyed him so much that in the end he had no choice but to get up and steal away to the cabbage-pile. A week later he was driven from this retreat by old Betty, who came and cut the very cabbage that sheltered him. Thereupon he returned to the seat on the hedge, and continued to use it until one morning he found a weasel curled up there. Then he forsook it for good.

That night, when considering where he should pass the coming day, his thoughts, as always in time of worry, turned to the hill, and at the approach of dawn, instead of heading for the farm, he set his face for Chapel Carn Brea. He was quite elated at the prospect of returning to the familiar upland; he even made up his mind where to sit; yet all came to nothing, for when he was a mile on the way another retreat won his favour and turned him from his purpose.

As he skirted the large pool on the Land's End moor his ever alert eyes fell on the tiny island in its midst; immediately there flashed on his mind an idea of the immunity from molestation such a retreat would afford. There, with the water around him, he felt that he would be safer than anywhere else; that neither fox nor cat, polecat nor weasel, would disturb him, nor man intrude; in short, that the islet offered the sanctuary he had often longed for and hitherto sought in vain. But there was one disadvantage, and a most serious one—the apparent impossibility of reaching the island without swimming. He knew from his experience at the mill-pool that no amount of shaking could dry a wet coat sufficiently to make sitting in it endurable for a whole day; and because of this he was on the point of abandoning the project and continuing his way, when, on second thoughts, prompted by the low state of the water, he decided to try whether he could reach the island by wading.

After looking round to see that he was not observed, he entered the pool and made straight for a rock where he meant to land before attempting to gain his goal, which lay just beyond it. But the water was soon so deep that at every step he dreaded finding himself out of his depth. Nevertheless, he was able to keep touch of the bottom until within some ten yards of the rock: there suddenly he had to rear on his hind legs to prevent his shoulders from being submerged. Most hares in this situation would have wheeled round and made for shore; but the jack was not so easily thwarted. A difficult situation called forth his resource: before you could count three, so quick was he to act, he was advancing on his hind legs over the rough bed, and he actually succeeded in gaining the rock without wetting more than a few inches of his coat. He stood a moment on the rock to shake the water from his chest and belly, then examined the strait between him and the island. It was far too deep to bottom, apparently far too wide to cross by a standing leap. But he meant to try. The worst that could befall him was a good drenching and the consequent abandonment of his plan. Twice he gathered himself to spring; as often he drew back; he was not satisfied with the hold of his front feet. A third time he gathered his strong hind limbs well under him, got a firm grip of the rock with his fore pads, launched himself with all the force he was capable of, and landed high and dry with a few inches to spare. After surveying his refuge, he leapt to the spot he had selected for his seat, and squatting close to the ground with his ears pressed close on his back, was indistinguishable from his surroundings.

The sudden disappearance of the animal which an instant before had been so very conspicuous was little short of magical; even when the sun rose it was difficult to pick him out, so happily did his colouring blend with the russet of the fern and the gold and grey of the lichens. One thing alone betrayed him, his eyes: they were wide open, maintaining their unbroken watch. For months they had kept vigil on cornfield, pasturage, and the enclosing hedges; now they scanned a waste of sullen mere and barren moor without sign of life save a wheatear flitting from stack to stack of the turf that dotted the heathery ground.

A harmless intruder was this frail bird; equally harmless the seagulls which came almost daily to drink and bathe and preen their plumage. At times the islet was ringed with their elegant forms: they might have been taken for the bodyguard of the hare, if there had been anything to suggest danger.

Dawn after dawn the hare stole back to his island retreat, where after awhile he began to throw aside his ordinary precautions and to relax his vigilance, passing the day in careless content. One noon he even grew so reckless as to abandon his usual wakeful position and rest on his side, with head and ears erect, his hind legs stretched out to their full length, and the white underfur exposed in a way that would have betrayed him to any prying eyes. The following day, soothed by the hot sun and the ripple against the bank, he actually fell so soundly asleep as to be insensible to his surroundings.

Alas, he was soon to be rudely apprised of the insecurity of his refuge, which was in fact an ancient holt of the otters that visited the pool. The awakening came on the nineteenth day in this wise. He was just back in the form casting his restless eyes about him as usual, when he saw something rise to the surface of the mere and almost instantly sink from view. The grey light and a mist prevented him from seeing clearly; yet he knew that it was an otter. At once he became alarmed for his safety, because he felt almost sure that the intruder would seek the island to couch on.

He was on the point of obeying his instinct to steal away whilst there was yet time, but irresolution held him back. He half rose; he resettled himself; he wavered again, and finally decided to await the issue. There he sat, watching and hoping that the creature would seek harbourage in the reeds beyond the spot where he had seen it. Minutes passed without a sign, he thought that his hopes were realised; he had almost ceased to scan the pool, when to his dismay the otter rose with a snort within a few yards, and lay motionless with his black bead-like eyes fixed on the island. It was a trying moment for the hare; had he moved ever so slightly the otter must have seen him, but he remained as rigid as the rock beside him; even his nostrils were at rest.

Presently, shaking the water out of her ears, the otter dived, only, however, to reappear with an eel in her mouth and land where the only creek on the islet had often invited her. Scarcely more than her length from the hare she lay down at full length with her head towards the water, and, holding the prey firmly between her fore paws, proceeded to devour it. Her wet coat gleamed when the sun rose across the level waste marking moor and pool with the shadows of the turf-stacks, yet the otter took no notice of the unfriendly rays; she was too much engrossed with her prey. Once she looked up, but no noise had attracted her; the slicing and champing of the flesh by her sharp white teeth was the only sound of that hushed hour. When she had eaten part of the fish, she dropped the remainder, advanced a few inches into the water and washed her muzzle with her great splayed foot, interrupting her ablutions to listen momentarily to the faint echo raised by a train of pack-mules. Then she returned to the islet and rolled on the fern. Now this way, now that, the long sleek creature turned and twisted, approaching dangerously near the little knoll against which the hare was pressed so close as to look scarcely more than half his size. At last, having dried her coat, she sought a clump of osmunda some five lengths from the hare, coiled herself up, and fell asleep.

Now again there was an opportunity for the hare to steal away: surely he would take advantage of it. But no; rather than run the risk of awakening the otter and being pursued, he decided to wait till twilight should call his enemy away and leave the way clear for him to effect his escape. So he sat watching the flank of the otter rise and fall, his gaze never shifting, even when a cormorant rose close to the island and looked at him with its green eyes before resuming its fishing.

Meanwhile the otter lay unconscious of the presence of the bird; but towards sundown the scream of a gull, and again soon after, the croak of a raven caused her suddenly to stir and scan the moor in order to satisfy herself that there was no cause for alarm. A glance telling her that all was well, she immediately lowered her head and dropped off again. The raven that had alighted close to the pool remained till near roosting time, and then flew away in the direction of the cliffs.

The bird was still in sight when an altogether unlooked-for intruder arrived. An old man with a dog at his heels came on the moor driving two donkeys to fetch turf; whilst he was loading the panniers from one of the stacks the terrier trotted to the pool to drink. There he hit the scent left by the otter at dawn. In an instant he was all excitement; being as intelligent as he was keen-nosed, he concluded that the otter must be lying on the island, and his one thought was to get at it. He entered the water and struck out as fast as he could swim. The otter, startled out of her sleep by a shout from the man, was at once on the alert, and when the dog drew near she slipped into the water; but the dog had seen her. Then a strange thing happened; the cormorant chancing to rise in the line of pursuit, the terrier took up the chase of the bird as if ignorant of the change of quarry. His master of course recalled him; he swam to shore; and immediately he landed, the otter, who was watching from the reeds, returned to the island, reaching it in one long dive. She landed at the creek as before, and crouching through the fern stole towards her lair.

She had taken but a step or two when she suddenly stopped, and turning her mask examined the ground to her left. She had caught the scent of the hare; she knew he was close by, and she was doing her utmost to descry him. She looked here, she looked there, and at last, as she was about to advance, she made him out. On the instant she sank slowly to the ground; she feared that quick movement on her part would put the prey to flight before she was free to pursue, for her shy nature restrained her from exposing herself to view of man and dog. So there she stayed, eyeing the timid prey which met her gaze with a frightened stare. Presently the man left with his donkeys. Now surely the otter would try and secure the prize. But no, she was in no hurry; the sun would soon be down, then she would secure him.

In that tense interval the hare again rehearsed, as he had done half a score times since he had been face to face with his enemy, the steps of his escape. The first leap he reckoned would land him on the far side of the islet, the next on the rock, a third in the water, on recollection of the depth of which he endured the agonies of a nightmare as in imagination he saw the ferocious brute overtaking him while he floundered; but the feeling passed, leaving him as undaunted as ever and determined to make a supreme effort to escape.

By this the sun approached the level of the moor; the gulls had left; the cormorant, which had stood and dried its wings on the rock, flew low over the lurid surface of the pool, looking black as the raven against the crimson disc: the actors in the impending tragedy were left absolutely alone. Soon, less than half the great orb remained above the horizon; in a few minutes, which seemed as many hours to the hare, it had sunk to the merest arc; then it disappeared.

This was the instant that the hare awaited; the otter knew it, and the hare saw that she knew it; the sudden gathering of her limbs proclaimed it. With a tremendous bound he was off, with the otter in hot pursuit. It was a close chase; for though the hare gained the rock a good ten feet ahead of the otter and increased his lead to fully fifteen at his next spring, the water, as he had foreseen, impeded his further progress so much that he seemed to be at the mercy of his swiftly advancing enemy. What floundering, what splashing by the hare! What ploughing of the water by the otter in her desperate haste! Foot by foot she gained till at last her nose all but touched his hind legs. It looked as if she must seize him; so she would have done but for a timely rock which gave the hare the foothold he needed. The spring he made from it was one of the longest of his life; it landed him well on to the shallows; two more leaps and he was on the heather, over which he sped like the wind. How good the herbage felt under his feet! Further pursuit was vain; yet the otter, maddened at the loss of the prey she had accounted hers, held on at her best speed to the corner of the pool before checking her steps to watch the hare. He stood awhile and returned her gaze. Then he shook his coat and resumed his way over the darkening moor.

CHAPTER VI
BACK ON CARN BREA

On leaving the moor the hare headed as if to return to Tregonebris, but in the dip below the stone-circle he suddenly changed his course and made straight for Brea. He had that instant formed the resolve to forage on the farm there and to harbour afterwards on his native hill. His panic pace, even more the staring eyes turned ever behind him, bespoke his nervous condition; but the farther he went the more composed he grew, and he was almost his normal self by the time he reached his destination.

There he roamed in search of food from pasture to pasture, wondering to see the change that had come over them since his early leveret days. Then the corn and the grass rose high above his head; he recalled how he had stood on his hind legs and looked over the array of ears; now there was not herbage enough to cover his pads. But despite the nakedness of the enclosures he experienced no sense of strangeness: the bushes on the hedges, the gates, the gaps and the linhay in the field beyond the old mine-heaps were the same as ever. He remembered them all, even the hole in the wall of the three-cornered enclosure; and through this, in the small hours, he squeezed his way to the turnip-field that runs like a narrow promontory into the waste. The sight of the turnips gladdened his eyes, for he had gleaned little on the closely browsed grass-land and was very hungry.

He at once pared the rind from one of the roots and began feasting on the succulent pulp. The stars shone bright, the fleecy clouds moved slowly, and the light wind scarcely breathed a sigh on the open waste where some curlews were whistling. The hare took no notice of their calls, but at the startled cry of a plover he at once sprang to the top of the wall, to learn, if he could, what had disturbed it. He scanned the face of the moor carefully without seeing any sign of a marauder, so at length returned to the half-eaten root and consumed it without further interruption.

The night was nearly gone before he withdrew, not following the way he had come, but leaping the wall and crossing the corner of the moor to the partly-upturned field. Here a plough in the furrow caught his eye and caused him to swerve from his path. Yet suspicious as he was of the plough he passed close to a bucket of mushrooms in the Five Acres, where he stood on a mound to gaze at the silent homestead and at Carn Brea before he set off for the hill. Then, as though the fading stars warned him of the need to hurry, he went at so brisk a pace that the noise of his pads on the bridle-track sounded quite distinct in the stillness of the dawn. At the foot of the long slope he quickly laid his maze; he threaded his way up and up past the Pilgrim's Spring almost to the chantry, and chose a seat amongst the bracken within a few yards of the spot where he was born.

Five months had passed since he sat there, but he felt quite at home. As the light grew, the outlook commanded a well-remembered prospect, albeit the vegetation had greatly changed. His young eyes had beheld it fresh and green; now all was sere and tinted with the colours of decay. Yet the herbage thus blended so wondrously with the russet of his coat that he was not to be distinguished from his surroundings. He seemed a part of the rich mantle which draped the giant shoulders of the hill down to the very verge of the farm, where all was grey and sombre save the bright gold of the sycamore by the dairy window.

Presently the farmer crossed the yard to the shed for the oxen and drove them along the lane to the half-ploughed field, followed by the watchful gulls, which came flying in from the cliffs in such numbers that the long furrow in the wake of the plough was soon white with their forms.

The hare was an interested spectator of all this movement; indeed everything that moved claimed his notice; not a leaf of the sycamore fell but it caught his eye. Stirred by association, old memories, too, came flocking back; once more he was a tiny leveret listening to the whispered monition of his mother, "Sit still, dears, till I come back"; once more he was sitting beside his little sister hearkening to the voices of the night that always died away before the footfall of their mother broke the silence of the dawn and set their hearts aflutter with delight. Then, though he strove to repress all sinister recollections, he rehearsed the visit of the vixen; a glint of the pool on the distant moor called up the horrors of the previous day.

But the most trifling incident diverted his attention; soon he was occupied in watching a red admiral which had settled on a bramble leaf and kept opening and shutting its gorgeous wings, as if for his distraction.

So hour after hour passed in the warm light that bathed the hill and touched with a velvety softness even the old chantry and the granite boulders, till at length the sun sank behind the sea, leaving plain and upland to the mystery of night and the glories of the full moon.

That day was the harbinger of a lovely St Martin's summer, during which the hare greatly enjoyed sitting on the hill and wandering over the lowland. It would have been a perfect time but for the abundance of the gossamers; they floated from every blade and spray and clung to his legs and chest, even to his face, causing him much annoyance. He was very nice as to his person; he could not rest unless his coat was free of everything that adhered to it, and it was a tedious business getting rid of the gossamer threads; indeed, it took him so long that he had to return earlier than usual so as to finish the grooming before daybreak, lest the movement of his pads and tongue, which served as brushes and sponge, should betray him to his enemies.

The welcome after-summer lasted a full fortnight, and was abruptly terminated by sea-fogs, that came rolling in from the Atlantic and enveloped the land as with a dense pall. Much as the hare had disliked the gossamer webs he disliked the fog still more, not only because it shut out the view and the light of the sun and the moon, but—what was much more serious—because it afforded cover to the foxes, who moved about as fearlessly by day as by night.

These prowlers became a positive trouble; scarcely a day passed but at least one went by; amongst them a big grey fox, whom he had never seen before, but of whom he was to see more than he liked in the terrible winter that followed. Yet close as these marauders approached the seats, they never discovered the hare.

In fact, the time of chief danger was the night. He was abroad then, but it was impossible to see more than a few yards ahead, so that once he almost ran into the farm cat in the mushroom field; two nights later he brushed close past a badger that was stretching itself against the upright of a cromlech. However, no harm ensued; for the hare leapt aside and was lost to sight in the fog as effectually as if he had been covered with a mass of cotton wool.

He got glimpses of other animals in his wanderings, though so vaguely that he failed to identify them. Moreover in the strange conditions the hare himself sometimes proved a terror to creatures he stumbled on, causing a hedgehog to curl up in affright on the Five Acres, and scaring a heron out of its senses on the moor beyond. The fog was as impervious to scent as to sight, and he was on his victims before they heard him, for the fog deadened all sound, of footfall, of bird cry, even of the great foghorn on the Longships, which sounded like a penny trumpet.

But of all the ills attendant on those ceaseless mists, the one which caused the hare most discomfort was the moisture that collected on the herbage and dripped on his back as he sat in the form. Two days he endured the misery; then he left the comfortable seat for the shelter of the fallen masonry of the chantry, and sat cheek by jowl with an enormous toad who resented his company till he got to understand and like him.

C. Reid.] [*To face p. 84.*

"Grey Fox."

On the fourth day, however, that the hare saw the great bank of fog come moving landwards from the sea, to the joy of man and beast an easterly wind set in which banished the fog and dried the sodden herbage, rendering the form habitable again. It was a keen, biting wind, but the hare felt no inconvenience. One sign of the cold snap was the red shawl in which the farmer's wife rode to market; another, quite as unmistakable, was the advent of the woodcock, whom the hare found sitting near the seat two days later. The stranger was unlike any bird he had seen; it had rich brown plumage beautifully pencilled, a very long bill, and soft black eyes which looked fearlessly into his. The hare, unobservant though he usually was of such matters, could not help seeing that it was very jaded and weary; and weary it might well be, for it had but just accomplished its long flight from Heligoland.

Two days before it had harboured in its native forest by the Baltic, awaiting the fall of night to begin its journey to the unfrozen West. When the moon showed above the ghostly steppe, the bird had risen over the snow-laden pine-tops and, mounting to a great height in company with a score others, set out for the hospitable land beyond the seas. The wind was favourable; bight, lagoon, and island marked the way, till the glimmer given out by a lighthouse—a glimmer that grew brighter and brighter—told that their mid-journey resting-place had been reached. They hid till night; then they rose again and resumed their flight beneath the starry vault.

No sound of earth reached the high region where they moved; their own faint wing-beats alone broke the silence through which hour after hour the wedge-shaped line pressed on till the vast silvery ocean that had lain outspread beneath them gave place to a sombre plain relieved only by the glow-worm light emitted by town and city far below.

Soon as remembered haunts were reached the little flock began to break up: now one, now two, and after a long interval, four birds forsook the line; others followed, so that when a second ocean showed on either side the narrowing land, only three remained. But the little remnant still sped on, nearer and nearer to their destination at the end of the promontory. Two dropped into Golden Valley, and the remaining woodcock reached Carn Brea alone. Little wonder, then, that he was very tired; yet so soon did he recover from his fatigue that when dusk fell he rose without an effort, and, skimming the slope, passed over Brea Farm and the now empty turnip-field to the boggy feeding-ground beyond.

Daybreak found hare and woodcock back in their places on the hill; and for three days they kept company there, or rather till the afternoon of the third day, when the wind veered back to the old quarter, beating with such violence on the face of Carn Brea that the hare could not endure it, and stole to sheltered quarters on the southern flank of the hill. There, with his back to a furze-bush, he sat watching the withered grasses of the foothills swept by the hurricane and the low wrack driven past close overhead. The wind fell at sundown, but rose again later and blew with such vehemence that the hare, who was foraging at Boscawen-Un, could scarcely make headway against it. Once he was actually brought to a standstill, and when crossing Brahan Moor on his way back it was all he could do to keep his feet. By the time he got to the form he was so wearied out by the incessant buffeting that whilst listening to the shriek and sob of the wind he fell asleep, and—a thing he rarely did—dreamt.

In his dream he saw as if with his eyes, so vivid was the presentment, a wood devastated by storm; at its foot—for the trees covered a long declivity—a curving strand and a raging sea in which living things struggled to reach the shore. Night changed suddenly to day: as suddenly the scene changed from falling trees and breaking waves to wind-swept foothills, up which, nose to ground, a brindled lurcher ran with incredible swiftness— and the foothills were the foothills below him, the lurcher was the farm dog from Boscawen-Un; the trail it followed was his own trail. His wide-open eyes beheld every twist and turn of the dog's advance without suggesting danger, till the enemy was almost within springing distance; then consciousness returned, and at a bound the affrighted creature cleared the bush and fled up the hill. He soon outdistanced his pursuer, fleet-footed though she was, reached the crest, swerved and ran with the gale at his back till within sight of Caer Bran. After coming so far he wished to satisfy himself that the dog still pursued. The wind lashed his face and beat down his ears; it threatened to blow him off the wall he stood on; but he held his ground and looked along his trail.

So had he often stood when followed by foxes, but never once did he get a glimpse of them: one and all recognised the uselessness of trying to overtake him, and relinquished the chase. He was now to learn that a dog will persist though success seems hopeless, for soon he saw the lurcher coming on at a pace that filled him with consternation. At once he became concerned for his safety, but not an instant was he at a loss where to go.

A naked lane ran down the long slope to Boswarthen Farm, and the hare struck into it in the hope that the gravelly track, holding little or no scent, would render further pursuit difficult if not impossible. The lane, which winds considerably, ends at a gate; under this he passed to the fields, skirted the homestead, and finally reached Johanna's Garden, where, after confusing the trail, he lay down in a furrow between two ridges of the upturned ground.

He had hopes of having defeated or disheartened his pursuer, yet it was in a fever of anxiety that he watched the gate under which he himself had crept.

His suspense was short, for soon to his horror a fox-like snout and long red tongue showed beneath the lowest bar. The next instant the lissom beast forced her way beneath it to the field. She at once picked up the line and followed it to the far corner near the old seat where the hare had leapt on the wall and walked along the rude coping-stones before leaping back and squatting near the medlar. Carefully and not without difficulty the lurcher followed the scent to the last of the stones, naturally thought that the hare had gone on, and dropped to the oat stubble, but finding no trace of scent, recognised her mistake. Then back she leapt to the wall, with wondrous ease considering its height; and though she could hardly keep her feet for the gale, she stood there all excitement, scrutinising the ploughed ground with eager eyes. She searched every furrow without descrying the hare; the leaves that whirled about him baffled her.

Though she failed to find him, she was so convinced he was there that she sprang to the ground and began questing, beginning at the lower end and casting to and fro across the wind in the most leisurely fashion, as if she knew there was no occasion for hurry. She had drawn about a third of the field when the hare, seeing discovery was certain, slipped from his hiding-place and, crouching very low, stole towards the wall. He hoped to get away unobserved, but his hope was vain.

Just as he reached the ditch the lurcher espied him, and with a single whine started in pursuit. Her pace down the stubble was tremendous; she was not more than ten yards behind the hare at the badgers' sett in the hollow below. But on the opposing rise she lost ground. By the time she came to the big pasture where she had picked up the line at dawn, the quarry was out of sight. She was again running by scent.

Though the hare had won and maintained a lead of nearly a furlong, he was beginning to feel the strain of the chase, and anxiously consulted with himself about his safety. Two voices made themselves heard: the homing instinct kept urging him to return to the hills; the voice of self-preservation with even greater insistence whispered, "Seek the moor, there alone safety lies"; so towards Hal Kimbra moor he held on and on, till at last, from a bit of rising ground, he saw the bleak waste stretching away before him. The fear of being sighted and coursed on the level surface made him shrink from crossing it: his indecision, however, was only momentary; on looking back and seeing no sign of his enemy, he determined to commit himself, though not before foiling his trail.

Between him and the lip of the moor lay a tract of marshy ground dotted with rushes and coarse grasses. Here, with a view to checking his pursuer, he leapt from tuft to hummock and from hummock to tuft until he had confused his line. Then he continued on his way, heading for an outlying turf-stack which stood between him and the pool. In the teeth of the hurricane he made slow progress, but he reached it at length, and glad of the shelter it afforded he sat down on the lee side, facing the ground he had just traversed. Soon he saw the lurcher coming, and watched her anxiously as she stood on the brow of the rising ground scanning the moor. The moment she set foot on the marshy ground, where she was lost to view, he quitted his shelter and made for the pool. Many a time he had covered the intervening ground in a minute or two; but the wind seemed bent on arresting his progress; in his exhausted state all he could do battling against it was to make headway. At length he gained the pool, and there his heart fell, for between him and his goal, the islet, lay a stretch of raging water. He had not reckoned on that.

He was a miserable creature as he sat on the shore, looking now towards the islet, now back over the moor. He could see no hope; death stared him in the face in both directions; yet the instant he saw the lurcher coming he decided to entrust himself to the pool. Strangely enough, he did not wade in, but galloped a score yards along the strand and then cast himself into the hissing water, striking the spray from the surface. When he rose he struck out for his goal. He was hardly visible even on the crests of the waves; he was completely lost to sight when they broke over him; but he drew nearer and nearer to the islet, and after a terrible struggle at last landed at the otters' creek.

Great as was the hare's distress, the love of life was greater. Even in his extremity he was careful not to betray himself by any sudden movement to his pursuer, now at the side of the pool. For fear of detection, he stole from the water at a snail's pace and, so slowly that no eye on the shore would have been aware of any movement, sank down on the sodden fern. There he lay hour after hour whilst his persistent enemy circled the pool and ransacked the waste in search of him.

It seemed as if she could not wrench herself away. Once, indeed, she withdrew; but when near the turf-stack she suddenly turned and came back, though the gale raged more furiously than ever. On reaching the pool, she entered the water and stood staring at the islet. The hare observed her with feverish anxiety; he knew that his fate hung by a thread, and scarcely breathed. To the dog the spray-washed rock gave no sign of life whatever, yet it was long before she abandoned this last hope and finally withdrew. A more crestfallen creature than she looked it would be difficult to picture; her gait had lost all its briskness, her limbs relaxed, her ears drooped. Her disappointment overwhelmed her; for she had counted the quarry hers the moment she sighted it, and on the moor had felt absolutely certain of it.

The hare watched the retreating form of his enemy till it became a speck and finally disappeared from view. Then he rose, looked round to see that no other enemy was in sight, shook his coat, rolled where the otter had rolled, ensconced himself in the most sheltered spot his inhospitable refuge afforded, and there remained till night. It was pitch dark when he withdrew by way of the rocks he knew so well.

CHAPTER VII
FROM PILLAR TO POST

With its overcast sky and sombre landscape November opened true to its character of the black month. The clouds seemed to have conspired to shut out the sun; only at rare intervals did the patient orb find a rift, but when it did its rays lit up with intense vividness the spot they fell on: Brea farmhouse, a bit of the moor beyond, Sennen Church tower, a patch of ocean, the welter of surf about the Wolf. To all of these, as the shafts of light illuminated them, the eyes of the hare were irresistibly drawn. A week of gloom and gleam was succeeded by a day of startling clearness, with lowland pencilled out distinctly as on a map, a day when the sea came so near that far-off sails and even the unobtrusive isles of Scilly made their presence felt. This phenomenon boded rain, and one morning soon after dawn it fell, gently at first, violently on succeeding days, with a gradual, decided shifting of the wind from the north-west to the north-east, whence at nightfall it blew with wintry coldness.

Had it been a dry wind the hare would have enjoyed its keenness, but it brought showers of sleet which wetted him through and through, making his days miserable. At night also these showers greatly inconvenienced him, inasmuch as he had to be continually shaking himself or galloping to and fro on the moorland tracks to keep his coat dry when he should have been at his pasture. He disliked the sleet more than the rain, and the hail more than the sleet, for the stones beat in his face and eyes; worse still, they lashed his ears and made them burn as he sat in the form, when his body shivered with cold from the dampness of the underfur.

During this inclement time he continued to use the seat on Chapel Carn Brea, the retreat under the drooping fronds drawing him as did no other. True, he could have found shelter beneath the chantry, but since lying there he had seen Grey Fox brush close by the opening which was the only way out; from that moment he abandoned all idea of repairing thither again, for fear of being cornered. He did give a thought to the cave in Brahan Croft, but could not bring himself to sit there; to the hut by the fowling-pool and to the linhay on Brea Farm, which presented themselves to his mind, he had still greater objection; whilst the rabbits' holes which proffered their shelter were altogether beneath his dignity, and indeed against his nature, to which no other roof but the sky was acceptable.

At last he had to abandon Chapel Carn Brea, on account of the water which lodged in the form and rendered it untenantable.

It was in pouring rain that the hare ransacked the country in search of new quarters, which he at last found in a plantation on the western slope of Sancreed Beacon. On reaching it, he remained awhile on the outskirts hesitating to commit himself to such a strange place, for so the wood with its array of trees seemed to him after the naked hills and barren moorland he was alone used to. Presently, with tremulous steps, he moved in and looked about him for a suitable seat. In selecting it he showed that he had his wits about him, for the spot he chose was as free from the drippings of the pines as any within his ken. After scratching a slight hollow amongst the fallen needles, he sat with his face to the hill taking in his surroundings. No undergrowth impeded his view, nothing save the stems and a tree or two blown down by the gale.

He soon felt at home, for the spirit of the place soothed him and banished the sense of strangeness. At first the fall of a pine-cone would startle him; by and by he took no more notice of it than he had of the popping of the furze-pods in the heat of August. He loved to listen to the soughing of the wind in the lofty tops, where the goldcrests were to be seen flitting to and fro. He believed them to be his only neighbours, till one night, just as he had risen, an owl came to the mouth of the hole in the next tree and called. The cry caused him to start, but at sight of the bird he regained his composure and finished stretching himself; in future if he happened to be by when the owl hooted, he did not even trouble to look up. One day was monotonously like another, so much so that the visit of a woodpecker, or the arrival of a wood-pigeon, was quite an event. Small wonder then that the hare, with his hermit-like tastes, felt happy in this peaceful solitude, and soon abandoned all thought of the intruders his imagination had conjured up.

Yet, before many more dawns had broken, the wood was visited by a pine-marten, a dangerous marauder, who resembled the hare in this respect that she too was the sole survivor of her kind. She came early; the stars had hardly begun to pale when, with scarcely a rustle to announce her coming, the hare saw her making as straight towards him as the trees permitted. Indeed, she threatened to overrun him, but stopped a dozen yards away near a patch of gaudy orange-red fungus, and sat scratching an ear till a shout from the glebe farm suddenly arrested her attention. At the sound she stood erect and listened with ears acock. She was an elegant creature with a bushy tail, resembling, save for her dark-brown colouring, a dwarf fox; and, like reynard himself, the moment she was satisfied that the shout, twice repeated, was not the hue and cry that had pursued her again and again, she relaxed her tense attitude and fell to play. She ran with bewitching grace and activity along the trunk and branches of a fallen tree, rested at the end of the longest branch, and, after brushing a feather from her muzzle, renewed her frolics, as if for the hare's entertainment. Then back she jumped to the ground, sprang to the nearest bole, climbed up and up, was plainly visible at the dome against the now reddening sky, and finally lay at full length on a horizontal branch scanning the scene below. Her quick eyes were everywhere—now on the jackdaws astir on the church tower, now on a labourer faring to work, now, as the light grew, on the vessels wind-bound under St Michael's Mount, and presently on the sun when its bright face showed above the Lizard and laid a golden pathway across the waters of the bay. Soon the rays fired the pine-tops, and turned to brightest crimson the tongue of the marten as she licked her glossy forelegs and buff-coloured breast. When she had finished grooming herself she lay awhile with her head between her paws, blinking and enjoying the genial warmth that dried her coat, and at last sought the deserted hawk's nest in the fork, where she had often curled up during her forays.

Her fastness was in the Land's End cliffs. Never was castle wall so stately or so majestic as the mural face of the precipice that furnished her a refuge some thirty feet above the Atlantic, whose roar was her lullaby.

R. H. Preston & Sons.]   [To face p. 100.

MOUNT'S BAY FROM THE BEACON.

There she slept away most of the hours between grey dawn and night. Awakened either by the scream of homing seafowl or by the level rays penetrating her lair, she watched through the narrow portal of her retreat the sun set, the glow die out of the west, and darkness spread over the face of the waters, before sallying forth to execute the raid she had planned. She was the wiliest of marauders, pilfering here to-night, elsewhere to-morrow, and, save that she avoided Boscawen-Un—the lurcher's home—ranging in all directions. She took toll of seafowl on the dizzy ledge, she robbed the farmers' henroosts and beehives, she stripped the squire's strawberry beds and plundered the crabber's bait, hang it where he might. Few places were inaccessible to her; she was as much at home on the crags of the Kites' Carn as on the loftiest pine of Sancreed Beacon.

It was a wonder that those quick eyes of hers had not descried the hare, but probably that was owing to the shouts which distracted her attention just as her gaze was being directed towards the spot where he sat motionless. As for the hare his eyes never left the strange creature. Her character he had read at sight. He read it in the feather on the muzzle, the blood-stain on the whiskers, and above all in the apprehension she showed on hearing the shout. To his view that was an infallible sign of a felon. He was glad when she ascended the tree and the length of the long stem separated them, for he believed that the marten had seen him and might have pounced on him at any moment. As he was far from being assured that she would not attempt to get at him before the day was out, he made a point of keeping awake and on the look-out for sign of movement in the eyrie between him and the blue vault.

Higher and higher rose the sun, flooding the hill with light, warming the resinous trees and filling the wood with their fragrance. But for the cold nip in the air it might almost have been a summer's day. One less suggestive of evil happening could not be; yet the first act of a tragedy of which the wood was to be the theatre was being enacted less than a furlong away, where two weasels were pressing a rabbit from gallery to gallery of its burrow. No hope for the defenceless thing lay there, still less in the wood across which it presently came loping with fateful laboured movement. A look of entreaty appeared in the rabbit's starting eyes when it saw the hare, but the doomed creature did not stop. On, on it struggled, followed still by the murderers, the two puny, lithe, fiendish-looking weasels.

The sight of these bloodthirsty miscreants stirred the hare to fury; scarcely had they passed when he rose and stamped with his hind feet: surely not to warn his own kind, it could not be that; it was his protest, his poor, ineffectual protest, against the outrage.

Intent on their quarry, the weasels gave no heed, but the owl looked out of its hole to learn what ailed its exemplary neighbour, and the marten peered over the edge of the nest to ascertain, if possible, the cause of the disturbance. She saw nothing of rabbit or weasels, for the trees hid them from sight, but she had an uninterrupted view of the hare, and at once was all excitement at the prospect of an unexpected feast. Though she had tasted hare once and only once, the memory of the delicious flavour remained, and she had often longed to taste it again. So eager was she that she could not take her eyes from off this unlooked-for prize; even the death-squeal of the rabbit which presently rent the air did not distract her gaze. After a while she lay down again, but not to sleep. She spent the rest of the day planning the capture of the hare, interrupting her deliberations only to rise every now and then to assure herself that the quarry was still below.

Far different had been the effect of that despairing cry on the hare. It left him disquieted and unnerved, with but one desire, to get away at the earliest possible moment from the wood and the murderer up above whom he had surprised in the act of looking down at him. Short as the day was, he thought that it would never end; and the moment the sun dipped below the plain he stole away noiselessly as a ghost, ascended the opposite hill, made along the high ridge, passed the earthworks, crossed the old camp on Bartinney and came to the chantry, where he stood awhile with his face towards the sunset. He seemed to be watching the expiring effort of day, but he was really considering where he should forage, above all where he should sit, on the morrow. He had no wish to sit on the hill; he wanted to get farther away from the wood than that; farther from its horrid association with blood. He thought of the island; he thought of a place that had once taken his fancy on the cliffs; he thought of Sennen Dunes, and in the end decided to seek a form there. The moment he had made up his mind he glanced along his trail, and, descending the hill, set out across the lowland.

That back look told that he had the pine-marten in mind; and well he might, for she was no mean enemy. She had watched the hare leave the wood, but so great was her dread of man that she feared to follow till the dusk deepened. As soon as she dared, however, she came down from the tree and took to the trail, following it up the long slope and along the heights past the Liddens to the chantry, where, with her breath coming quickly, she stood eagerly scrutinising the hillside and the flooded lowland all agleam in the moonlight. Her coat was wet from the heavy dew, but she was too preoccupied to shake it; all her senses were in her eyes searching in vain for the quarry now far away in the midst of that water-logged moor. When she saw no sign, her heart sank; she was at a loss to know what to do. She was very loath to abandon the quest, but the dread of a blank night if she persisted weighed with her, so she presently forsook the trail on which she had stood and disappeared into the night.

Meanwhile the hare, who had reached the moorland farmstead he had made for, passed from one small enclosure to another, picking what little herbage he could find. With the help of the furze-shoots he managed to get his fill before leaving to roam for hours over the snipe-haunted waste. Hither and thither he journeyed, seemingly without any other object than to pass the hours away, going farther and farther from his goal, to which, however, he turned at the first crow of the crofter's cock, so that the somewhat stormy dawn found him ensconced in a shallow pit on the brink of the dunes. He had chosen wisely; the sand was dry, and the thick marram-grass screened him from the keen wind which tore the spindrift from the rollers that tripped and foundered on the strand.

Yet, comfortable though he was, his mind was ill at ease; he was haunted by the tragedy of the pinewood. He did all he could to deaden memory of the scream, but the cries of the gulls kept it alive till a peregrine shot into view and drove them to the cliffs: then it faded and left him at peace. Even now he dreaded falling asleep, for fear of being visited by nightmare; he fought against his drowsiness, but in vain; he had dropped off before the gulls returned. Neither marten nor weasel harassed his peaceful slumbers, rendered delectable by a vision of the strand up and down which he was speeding like the wind, not alone, but in company with mother and sister. It was a very vivid dream; he felt the breeze in his face, the shells under his feet; his happiness was complete. He was sorry to awake, but the presence of the beach cheered his disappointment as he looked forward to a good gallop on the smooth sand left exposed by the ebb. At earliest nightfall he left the form and in part realised his dream, tearing up and down the level foreshore and spurning the sand as he went. It looked as though he would never tire, his sinews seemed to be of steel; but at length he withdrew and betook himself to the feeding-ground.

Dawn after dawn he returned to the dunes. Dusk after dusk he enjoyed his gallop, till one night he discovered the cat and two kittens crouching beside the path he always left by. Then, rather than run the risk of capture, he decided to forsake the delightful spot and return to the hill. True to his resolve, he was at Carn Brea on the morrow, and to his joy found the seat much drier than he expected. Better, however, had he gone anywhere else, for as things chanced he was to be the harassed spectator of a terrible affray between his two most dreaded enemies, the final scene in the drama that began to unfold itself soon after he was ensconced.

The dawn was clear despite the grey sky, with only a belt of mist here and there on the lowland to interrupt his watch for the night-prowlers returning to their lair. The scanning of the moor was his constant practice, because of the haunting dread he had of being stumbled on by homing fox or fitchet; in fact, he never settled down with a feeling of real security until day had fully declared itself and driven all his persecutors to their retreats. Not a living thing showed at first; presently however his gaze was arrested by some animal that issued wraith-like from a patch of mist, and after crossing a wide strip of moor entered the croft bordering the "linhay" field. There he could see it as it threaded the stunted furze, though not plainly enough to make quite sure that it was a fox as he suspected. All doubt was removed when the creature, after being hidden by intervening bank and overgrown ditch, crossed the boundary wall and began stealing up the hill straight for the form. It was Grey Fox himself. It looked now as if the hare's forebodings were at last to be verified, but it was not so, for the brute entered the clump of tall furze midway up the slope and remained there.

The hare concluded that the fox had kennelled; he even judged him to be already asleep, so weary and exhausted did he look. But Grey Fox never thought of curling himself up; he was far too anxious for that; he was eagerly surveying the plain for sight of the enemy who had been pursuing him from farm to farm and moor to moor since midnight. He looked long without seeing aught, but he dared not compose himself to sleep. Instead he withdrew to the little grassy space behind the furze, where he kept walking up and down under the eyes of the hare, like a wild beast in a cage. "Strange behaviour this," thought the hare. "There's something very wrong with Grey Fox this morning. See how his flanks heave! what a mist his breath makes!" Presently the gaunt creature ceased pacing and lay down at full length, but after a few seconds he got up again and went back to the furze.

There he again watches the plain, where a speck scarcely discernible grows larger and larger, and tells him that the lurcher has recovered the trail she had temporarily lost, the trail he himself had left, and that the lifelong feud is on the point of settlement, for Grey Fox has made up his mind to have it out with his enemy. By this time the hare too has seen the dog, and whilst following her progress in the furze, wonders that the fox does not retreat whilst there is time. So excited does he become that he fain would warn the fox, but dares not; though more than once he is on the point of stamping his feet, he refrains. Meanwhile, the lurcher shows on the boundary wall, on which she stands and surveys the face of the hill. Her breath too comes quick, like jets of steam. She is wondering, as she gets no glimpse of the game, whether it is worth her while to go any farther, for twice before during the hare's absence from the hill she has hunted Grey Fox half the night, only to drive him to ground on the north side of Bartinney, where at this moment she thinks he is probably curled up in his inmost den, far beyond her reach. But such is her keenness that she cannot resist the burning, alluring trail, and leaping from the wall, she makes her way up the hill and enters the furze, where Grey Fox awaits her.

Without growl or snarl the fight begins. Except the violent shaking of the bushes, there is no outward indication of the terrible struggle that goes on. For a long while the hare, watching excitedly, sees nothing of the combatants save the white tip of the fox's brush, but anon they come into the open, where not a spray shuts out the view. They seem equally matched, because though Grey Fox leaps, now this way, now that, as if yielding to the lurcher's determined onslaught, he is not giving way: it is but his method of preventing the enemy from fastening on his throat. The quickness of his movements is wonderful, nor does he forget to use his jaws. See how he snaps! The strange noise is the clashing of his teeth when they fail to get home. The struggle is too furious to last: before the lapse of half an hour the life-long enemies lie exhausted on the ground, face to face with each other, their laboured breathing audible to the hare.

The fox when he recovers has no more wish to renew the fight than he had to begin it, but the lurcher's one thought is to destroy the hateful wild thing before her, or die in the attempt. Again they fight; only for a short while now; limb and wind are unequal to further effort; their exhaustion is complete. At last the lurcher recognises that to kill the fox is a task beyond her powers. After a time she staggers to her feet and looks into the eyes of Grey Fox, who has also risen. The meaning of the looks they exchange no pen can tell, unless it is that the curled lips and bare teeth bespeak undying hate. Then the lurcher withdraws, leaving the fox to himself. Reynard's ears are pricked, he is listening to the retreating footfall, and when the sound dies away he drags himself into the bushes.

There, screened from the light of the sun and the eyes of all observers, he sat and licked his wounds, interrupting the process only to rise and reconnoitre through an opening in one of the bushes. Though he saw nothing of the dog, the fears which urged him to withdraw became at last so insistent that he actually crept out in the broad sunshine and made for the earth. At once the hare was on the alert. His apprehension, however, subsided on seeing the crippled condition of his enemy, who was limping on three legs and had to pick his path. Soon the fox swerved to avoid a patch of broken ground within twenty yards of the form, and now he must pass close to its occupant. Discovery is certain, is imminent. The hare's scent betrayed his near neighbourhood; his conspicuous eye betrayed his person. Did the fox, ravenous though he was, attempt the capture of the prey? Not at all, he knew the futility of trying in his disabled condition. The situation was one that called for the exhibition of his powers of make-believe. His aim was to convince the hare that he had not seen him, and to this all his cunning was directed; he checked the working of his nostrils excited by the scent, he averted his glance and looking straight before his long nose, which was badly scarred, held on as though ignorant of the hare's presence, with the demeanour of a creature overwhelmed by misfortune. But the hare, every whit as crafty as he, had caught the glint of his eye, had observed the sudden arrest of the nostrils, had read his mind through and through, and before Grey Fox was abreast of the chantry had already made arrangements not to be at home when he called. An indescribable look came into the hare's usually impassive eyes as he thought of the disappointment that awaited reynard, on whose mask as he crossed the ridge played an expression of satisfaction at the prize that would be his before the moon was very much older. The prospect of the delicious feast forced the memory of the fight into the background; for the rest of the way he ran on four legs, and it was of the hare, not of the lurcher, he was thinking when later he fell asleep curled up in the innermost recess of his earth.

Meanwhile the hare, who had resolved to abandon the hill for a while, sat thinking over the question of a new seat. His mind once more ran over all the old forms, but in the end rejected every one of them for the untried retreat in the cliffs to which he had been on the point of going before.

That night he spent on the moorland, where—a most unusual thing—he did not encounter a single trail or hear a disturbing cry, though after his gallops he always stopped to listen. He looked the picture of attention, standing on knoll or barrow with his great ears raised to their full height to catch the voices of the wild. A few seconds only did he bestow on this duty; he was in too high spirits to give more. His exuberant energies called for vigorous exercise, and when he was not spinning along or hearkening, he skipped and frisked about like a frolicsome kid. He travelled miles and miles, "going all ways," so that midnight had long passed when he set foot on the strip of waste overlooking the sea. There he nibbled the herbage and ate all the blackberries he could find, shrivelled though they were. Rearing on his hind legs he stripped every bramble patch before crossing to the cliffs, where he dropped from terrace to terrace till he came to the spot at which he intended to sit.

But then a steep slope that still more took his fancy opened to his view. Though eager to reach it, he paused at the edge of the chasm that separated him from it; the turmoil of the water in the gully and the raging of the surge in the great cave to which the gully led disconcerted and checked him. After a moment's hesitation, however, he leapt the opening, gained the slope, and sat on a cushion of thrift overlapping the lip of the under-cliff. Within the ambit of his wanderings he could not have selected a more secluded spot. Man had never set foot there; save for the old fisherman who rested on his oars to gaze at the primroses, sea-pinks, and foxgloves that in their season decked this hanging garden, no human eye had seen its beauty. Even now the solitary furze-bush amongst the naked rods of the foxgloves was gay with blossom, for the slope fronted south and caught the sun. Sitting there the hare observed every living thing within his ken. He watched the gannets that sent the spray flying as they dived into a school of pilchards; he was interested in the cormorants that stood on the rock below and dried their outstretched wings; even the little companies of mullet did not escape him, when they came scurrying past the point and coasted round the tiny bay; and by such sights his attention was drawn, his curiosity excited, as he enjoyed the warmth of the sun that brightened the austerity of the cliff and sparkled on the wintry sea.

December found the hare using this retreat. All went well with him till one day in leaping the chasm he landed a little short and nearly fell back into the sea, but by great good fortune his hind feet, striking blindly for support, found foothold on a ledge. That saved him. The mishap was the result of carelessness, and afterwards, being cautious as to the place from which he took off, he cleared the opening with several inches to spare.

But he was never free from fear. One morning he had returned very early whilst the stars were yet bright; the cluster above the headland sparkled like a diadem. Towards this the eyes of the hare were directed, when one of the constellation was suddenly shut out by some dark object which was at first unrecognisable; by and by it turned; it was the pine-marten. The creature went as suddenly as she came, but soon reappeared on a narrow shelf of the headland, where she stood looking down at a chough some twelve feet below. Rapid in decision, the marten dropped with the intention of seizing and disabling the bird before it could take wing. The chough, however, was too quick and flew off, so the marten fell on the rocks, and failing to get the grip for which she strove frantically, tumbled head over heels into the boiling sea forty feet below. The hare thought that he had seen the last of this nimble enemy. He was soon to be undeceived, for presently to his surprise her mask, then her whole body showed above the edge of the chasm where she sat examining the slope. She kept looking in the direction of the furze-bush as if she saw something of interest there, then suddenly turned, leapt the opening without an effort, and disappeared along the very ledge from which she had tried to drop on the back of the chough.

The visit of the marten greatly disquieted the hare. He believed that if she had discovered him he could hardly have got away. So the question, Should he abandon the retreat? confronted him. He was loath to leave, but in the end decided to forsake the spot, because he felt that even if the marten did not return, he would enjoy no peace through fear that she would. It was an unfortunate resolve; had he decided otherwise, he might have avoided the most harassing trials of his life.

CHAPTER VIII
THE GREAT WINTER

After leaving the form the hare kept loping to and fro on the strip of waste by the cliffs. No tempting bit of herbage detained him; he nibbled neither leaf nor spray; his movements were as aimless as they could be. He was in a quandary; he did not know where to turn because he did not know where he was going to sit, though it had occupied his thoughts since the withdrawal of the marten.

Of the many spots that occurred to him not one offered especial attractions like the hill, which kept presenting itself to his notice, without however winning him to it. And this is not to be wondered at, in view of the fear he had of being waylaid and gobbled up by Grey Fox if he ventured there. Nor was his fear groundless. Grey Fox had haunted the hill in the hope of securing what he esteemed the titbit of the wild. Day after day in the half light of the morning and in the dusk of the evening he crouched in one spot after another beside the path by which he thought the hare might leave or return, persisting in the quest until he had completely ringed the form with his ambuscades and satisfied himself that the hare was no longer using it.

At last he went to examine the seat: it was cold and scentless, and he realised what a fool's business he had given his best energies to. Standing there he chided himself for throwing away so many precious hours, above all for being outwitted by a hare. Scathing was his self-reproach, yet brief, for Grey Fox wasted little time in vain regrets. He wanted to come to a settlement, and was concerned to know where the sly hussy of a grass-feeder had betaken herself. For a moment he stood with his bluish-green eyes fixed on vacancy, lost in thought, as if wondering where she could be, then stole down the slope, trailing his great brush as he went. He was abandoning the hill.

This was on the night that the hare narrowly escaped falling into the gully, so that after all puss might have safely returned instead of racking his poor brain over a new seat. In the end he found one on the moor, atop of a grassy mound which had once taken his fancy as he passed. From the slightly raised station he commanded a wide outlook across the waste, whose monotony the pool with its yellow reeds served in some measure to relieve. The moor, drear and barren though it was, furnished hospitality to a few migrant birds; a jack snipe fed within a dozen yards of the hare, a flock of golden plover was on the ground out of his ken beyond the pool. Later, eleven in all, they flew with musical whistlings over the reeds and across his front. Nor were these the only feathered visitors. Soon, as the weather grew colder, duck, widgeon, and teal visited the pool to feed, arriving at nightfall and leaving at dawn for the sea, where they rested through the day. Their line of flight was only a little wide of the mound, and the hare was always back in time to see the skeins go past. More than once too he caught sight of the dusky forms of otters stealing back to the cliffs; they were returning from a raid on the waterfowl.

But nothing is of long continuance in the wild. The visits of the duck were abruptly terminated by the freezing of the pool, and a phalarope, whom the lone water had attracted, was driven away at the same time.

The plover remained, the snipe foraged along a runnel fed by a warm spring, but the heath was rendered uninhabitable for the hare by the piercing wind, against which the withered grasses of the mound afforded no protection. He endured the discomfort for some days, then as it became unbearable he forsook the spot and returned, not without misgivings, to the hill. But Grey Fox was still present to his mind; he approached with the utmost caution, carefully shunned the old form, and sat at a spot midway between it and the chantry.

In this higher station, however, he found effectual shelter from the wind, though its whistling sounded menacingly close, especially when it rose, as towards night it often did, to a shriek.

In its shrillest notes the north-easter was almost articulate; it seemed to sound a warning of the bitter weather to come. For the cold was no mere snap like the previous visitation; it was, as the old tenant of Brea Farm foresaw in the red sunsets and dead set of the wind, the beginning of a season of unusual severity. The flocks of redwings and fieldfares which had sought the westernmost angle of the land found the exposed fields as hard frozen and inhospitable as those they had fled from. In the sheltered valleys alone, when the abundant crop of haws along the hedgerows had been consumed, were they able to pick up a living and find what was almost as necessary as food, a roosting-place out of the eye of the wind. The blackthorn brakes, every branch of the holly and the furze, any bush screened by ivy, were all occupied at night by thrushes, mistle-thrushes, blackbirds, linnets, and finches, whilst bevies of larks slept on the ground below.

Remarkable as was that December for the inrush of common birds, it was scarcely less so for the rarer visitants: a bittern harboured in the reed-bed of the pool, a gaggle of bernicle geese haunted Porthcurnow Cove, five wild swans sought a refuge in the waters of Whitesand Bay, whilst quite a number of Dartford warblers and firecrests found sanctuary in the snug brakes of Golden Valley. There was not a sheltered bottom or bay without its feathered guests. On the other hand, not a bird was to be found on the hills: Sancreed Beacon, Caer Bran, Bartinney, were deserted by every living thing save hibernating adder, slow-worm, and newt; the old toad and the hare were the sole tenants of Chapel Carn Brea.

Protected by his thick winter coat the hare was able to withstand the nipping frosts that blackened all but the hardiest and most unpalatable herbage, to which he was for the most part now driven for support. He fed on furze and lichens and no longer looked forward to the joys of pasturing time. Instead, his thoughts turned to the nights of plenty, to remembered feasts on tender corn and sweet trefoil, to banquets on fragrant thyme and juicy sow-thistles, to titbits like the pinks, above all to the musk, the tastiest morsel that his beats had furnished. He never wearied of dwelling on the appetising list; he would rehearse it again and again, and wonder whether the good things of the honeysuckle time would ever come again. He quite lost himself in these reveries; the hissing of the wind, even the ring of the horse's hoofs that broke in on his musings as the farmer rode away to market, failed to disturb them.

He was trying to recall the flavour of dandelions as he dreamily watched man and horse cross the lowland which seemed to shrink and cower beneath the low-hanging sky. Clouds, grey and depressing, spread from horizon to horizon save in the south-west, where at close of day after day the red sun emblazoned the heaven, and for a brief while bathed ocean and promontory with its cheery rays. They were especially pleasing to the hare, coming as they did between the dull day and the dark night when he wandered far and wide after pasture. Yet widely as he roamed he never came across the packs of stoats which the host of birds had attracted, nor—a thing that excited his surprise—once encountered Grey Fox.

Nevertheless he often thought of him, wondering what had befallen him: whether he had met his death from the lurcher or been expelled from the earth by the badgers and betaken himself elsewhere. Neither supposition was right. Like the stoat-packs, Grey Fox harboured in the valleys, attracted by the easily captured prey and making the most of his opportunity. It was well for him that he did. In the middle of December snow fell, shutting off food from the birds and causing all but the hardiest to perish of hunger.

It would seem that the wind had delayed the fall, for no sooner did it die away than the flakes began to descend, lightly at first, then close enough to hide all but the nearest objects, so that when at last they ceased, the land was covered to a depth of several inches. Spray and frond did not submit more passively to the fall than did the hare; in the end he was as completely hidden as a sheep in a drift. And like the sheep he had not to bear the weight of his covering, for the heat of his body thawed the snow round it, with the result that, when it froze again, a shell of ice was formed, thin indeed, yet able to sustain its load. For a while the hare was in complete darkness, but his breath presently melted the snow in front of his nostrils, forming a peep-hole through which he looked out on a world he could no longer recognise. His very threshold seemed strange; only the side of the near boulder with its streaks of yellow and grey lichens presented a familiar face.

The heavy fall had cleared the sky, whence a vast array of stars looked down on a world as hushed as the depths they lighted. A wondrous silence reigned over hill and plain, till it was broken in the dead of night by a vixen calling from beyond the farm. The penetrating cry had scarcely died away when from the distance came a faint response. On hearing it the vixen squalled again, and was answered from Bartinney.

Again the awful squall rang out; this time the reply rose from beside the rock near the chantry. The sharp yap, thrice repeated, made the hare tremble, and no wonder, for it seemed to him to proceed from the back of his snow-hut. Then he heard the muffled thud of approaching footfall, and the next instant the form of Grey Fox flashed by as he bounded down the hill straight for the curlew-moor, whence the vixen had called.

Perhaps it was as well for the hare that a vague fear, caused by the new element, had kept him to the seat, for had Grey Fox and his mate chanced on him before he was accustomed to the snow, the countryside might have known him no more.

But staying within his snow-hut was not without its drawbacks; he had to suffer for his inaction; his fore legs ached; his hind legs were gripped by cramp; even worse than that was the itching of his ears, which he was afraid to scratch for fear of bringing his house down.

Luckily these attacks came one at a time, until the hour before sunset, when they fell together and nearly drove him mad. The red sun that had previously been such a comfort to him, now seemed as if it would never go down and set him free to stretch his limbs and scratch his ears. But it sank at last, though a bit of the rim still showed when he burst out and made off like the wind. Beyond the chantry he pulled up; he would at last be rid of the itching in his ears; but the cramp threatened and sent him going again. So down the hill he tore, putting his feet into a blind hole and tumbling head over heels with the impetus of his rush. He was on his feet in a twinkling, and aided by the hairy soles of his pads, scurried over the frozen surface with singular ease towards the linhay field, where he began scraping the snow away to get at the herbage beneath. What little he found he ate ravenously, but there was not enough to stay his hunger, which he appeased with the shoots of the furze.

The light in the farmhouse window was yet burning when he ceased feeding and began wandering over the moor. He was not happy. The vague misgivings which had harassed him whilst in the form, the disquiet caused by ancestral monitions, became real fears when he recognised that he was leaving a trail easy to follow unless he confused it. Whereupon, coming to the end of the outward journey, he wove a maze of tracks amidst the scattered bushes, and the better to conceal the line by which he returned, crept along an overgrown ditch where only a practised poacher could have traced him. He roamed until day was about to break, and when the sun arose it found him sitting by the spring near the Fairies' Green.

He was very tired, but afraid to drowse. Every moment he expected to see some enemy coming along his trail, and for hours he kept watch on the white plain till sleep claimed him, leaving his sentinel senses on guard. No moving objects, however, fell on his sight, nothing save the waste of snow and the vapour over the spring: no sound smote his ears except the purl of the rill and the faint tinkle of the ice-crystals on the sedge, so that—a most unusual occurrence—he did not awake till the sun was about to go down and it was time to think of leaving the form. After an uneventful night's wandering he returned to the seat, and would have continued to use it had not the wind risen again, rendering the situation so inclement that he had no choice but to go.

His intention was disclosed by his carelessness on quitting the form. Instead of bounding from it, as was his usual practice, he simply stepped out, leaving tracks that a child might have traced home, and leaping across the runnel he rolled on the green, a thing he would never have done had he meant to come back. Very different was his conduct at dawn in the field by Johanna's Garden. He crossed and criss-crossed his tracks before springing on to the hedge, and from that into the garden, where, after two of his longest leaps, he squatted some dozen yards from the medlar.

Yet, carefully as he had concealed his approach, he could not conceal his person. Indeed, he looked very conspicuous on the surface, which, if not quite flat, was only slightly wavy from the ridge and furrow beneath. Perhaps he knew that snow threatened, and relied on it to hide him. However that may be, the flakes began to fall thickly soon after he had settled down, and when they ceased he was as effectually covered as he had been on the hill. Then the sun came out, turning countryside and garden into a glittering fairyland.

The resplendent enclosure seemed to be crying out for some creature to enjoy its delights, when suddenly, without a sound to announce their approach, two full-grown stoats appeared on the wall by the badgers' creep and stood looking down at the snow. They were not seeking the tracks of the hare, they were not hunting, they were abroad simply for the snow, and the next instant they sprang to the ground and began rolling over one another, uttering a happy chuckling noise the while. On separating they wallowed in the snow, as if they could not get enough of the joy of it. But all at once they rose to their feet, raised their long necks and listened; an unusual sound had alarmed them. It was only the noise made by the snow that fell from the overladen branches, and the instant they discovered the cause, they resumed their romps, twisting and turning like snakes and time after time leaping into the air. The height they jumped was quite surprising; almost eerie was their speed as they galloped over the snow.

The hare watched them at their games without serious alarm, he was almost interested in their movements, when presently they fell to "hide and seek," but the moment they gave over playing and began searching the furrows for mice he was in dread lest in their tunnellings they should bump against and discover him. Hence he kept an anxious look-out, and when a long interval passed without a sign of them he suffered agonies of fear. Even when they did show, it was not much he saw, just their heads, and that only for a moment or two. As they approached, however, he could discern the slight heave of the snow that attended their progress. Presently up popped the head of the nearest, within a few yards, and when it was withdrawn up popped the head of the other in the adjacent furrow, only to disappear again as the two made their way towards the gate. The hare, more and more terrified, awaited their return, and before long saw the snow lift along the furrow next the one in which he sat. Then the head of the stoat appeared, but was instantly drawn back as a dark shadow fell on the snow.

It was a kite who, in her station high overhead, had espied the stoats, and carrion-feeder though she usually was, had come after them. For the bird, ravenous with hunger, was forced to get anything she could secure, and from the medlar-tree on which she alighted watched the snow eagerly for sign of the prey. The stoats, aware of her presence, lay as still as death. An hour, two hours passed, then the bigger stoat cautiously raised his head to reconnoitre, and on seeing that the kite was still there, as cautiously withdrew it, hoping thus to escape her attention. But in vain: nothing could escape the bird's fierce, searching eyes. She instantly glided to the spot, and with the outstretched talons of her great yellow feet kept grabbing at the heaving snow, yet always too far back to secure the retreating stoat, for he moved with amazing rapidity and never once stopped nor showed his head. Of course the kite could move as fast as he, and ought to have caught him; indeed she would have done, had she not been so stupid as to keep striking just behind him. A more exciting chase could hardly be witnessed; again and again the kite seemed to have learned wisdom and to be about to close her talons on the stoat, but as often failed, and when at last she struck directly above the stoat he had gained the drift by the hedge and was too deep for her to reach. Thus the pursuit came to an end, but not the incident, for from his vantage ground the stoat chattered insults at the bird as she flew back to the tree to await the appearance of the other stoat.

The second stoat, however, had peeped out during the chase and, seeing the way clear, ran to the near hedge, where she lay safe amongst the stones that once formed the walls of the cottage. Her tracks on the snow told of her withdrawal; but they had no message for the kite who, after watching in vain till the day was nearly gone, at last spread her wide wings and sailed away in the direction of the Kites' Carn. Lucky creature, thought the hare, whose eyes followed the bird's flight as far as the narrow peep-hole allowed, lucky creature to be able to glide through the air and avoid the drifts. The reflection came into his mind that night as he struggled through deep snow near High Down, whither he was attracted by the hawthorn bushes.

On reaching the bleak spot, he went from tree to tree gnawing the bark on the windward side, so that while he fed, his back was to the gale and his face in a measure protected from the driven snow. He seemed to prefer the rind on the upper part of the stem, for at each of the three bushes he stood on his hind feet and reached as high as he could, despite the swaying of the bushes under the gusts that shook them. The creaking noise they made formed a weird harmony with the moan of the wind, which was quite in keeping with the spirit of the haggard upland.

Soon the hare, unable to endure the bitter cold, forsook the down for the lowland and made for home. Home! Can it be said that he had ever had a home? The hill had perhaps the best claim, then there was the Fairies' Green, and the moor, but all of them too exposed for him now, hardiest of earth's children though he was. Privation, besides, had begun to tell on him, and in his weakened condition he turned from the wild to seek the protection afforded by man; so he was making for the homestead of whose daily life he had been so close an observer, striking through the blinding storm over field and waste as unfalteringly as though guided by some visible beacon.

In the midst of the great croft by Boscawen-Un stone-circle he became a prey to misgivings which caused him to stop and consider. "Is it safe," he asked himself, "to entrust myself so near to man?" Instantly from that mysterious second self of his came the answer, "Why not? Man has never injured you, never even sought you, though you have battened on his crops and taken of his best." Reassured by this thought he held on his course across the moors till abreast of Chapel Carn Brea, where he again paused. Dark though it was, thickly as fell the snow, he could discern the form of the great hill that had been to him like a second mother. If it be possible for beast to love a spot on earth, the hare loved the hill where he had been born and suckled, the hill which had sheltered him, the hill to which, in his trouble, he had always turned. He had never passed it by unregarded, he could not even now. But it looked ghastly and cold, it repelled him, Chapel Carn Brea repelled him as a dead thing once loved repels the living; so he averted his gaze and moved on towards the homestead. He followed the bridle-path all the way, but just before reaching the house he passed under the third bar of the gate of the rickyard, made his way between the turf and the furze-stack, and jumped on to the wall in their lee. There he sat between the stems of two elders, with his face to the farmyard, wondering what the coming day had in store for him. His heart was beating faster than its wont.

CHAPTER IX
PERIL OF DEATH

For some time the hare seemed to be the only living thing within the homestead: not a cry broke the silence till the finches and linnets roosting in the furze-rick, in the eaves and crannies of the buildings, and even in the buildings themselves, began to twitter, heralding with their low, sweet chorus the wintry dawn.

Presently too there was a sign of stir within the house: smoke rose from the chimney, now and again a spark with it, quenched immediately by the snowflakes which fell as close as ever, thickening the covering that lay like a robe of ermine on the yard, on the roofs of the house, sheds, barn, and the derelict pigeon-cote springing from its ridge.

But though the household was astir no one seemed disposed to venture out, till at last Andrew, the farm-hind, lantern in hand, appeared, his feet sinking deep at every step as he made for the cattle-stalls under the barn. The flame lit up his corduroys, his homespun jacket, and beardless chin; it faintly illuminated the mud wall on which his shadow fell; it dispelled the pitchy darkness of the byre, where with loud lowings ox and bullock greeted his entry. He was soon busy chopping turnips, whose fragrance spread around till it reached the hare and set him longing; then the munching of the cattle almost drove him beyond endurance; but he remembered that he was an outlaw, so he turned a deaf ear to the tantalising sound, though he could not help envying the beasts which he had hitherto pitied. By this the farmyard was wide awake; the inmates of every shed and pen clamoured to be fed; the bull bellowed, the horse whinnied, the pigs squealed, the geese cackled, the rooster crowed at the top of his voice, whilst the linnets, finches, siskins, a yellow-hammer and a snow-bunting looked mutely on, hoping not to be forgotten.

And so the hours of early morning passed, succeeded by a sunless forenoon and the dinner hour, during which the hare contemplated an act of unusual daring, nothing less than joining the three yearlings who were eating hay from a rack in the midst of the yard. After all, it did not seem a great thing to do. He had but to slip from the wall, steal a dozen yards or so over the snow, then the fodder would be his for the taking. Yet he could not do it; his wild nature restrained him. Once indeed he half rose, only, however, to settle down again and watch the yearlings empty the rack, which the man removed on returning from his dinner. As he carried it he chanced to look towards the hare, who, ever suspicious, feared that he was discovered. It was quite a critical moment to the wildling; had the man's eyes met his, had the man only stopped whilst gazing in his direction, he would have made off: luckily, neither event befell, so that the hare, who had gathered himself ready to spring, relaxed his muscles and remained. The incident, however, left him somewhat disquieted, till a wren foraging in the elder diverted his thoughts; then he became composed and followed the movements of the man with the same unconcern as before.

Yet, fearful as he was of man's gaze, he was able to disregard sounds that would have made fox, marten, and stoat cower and slink to cover; he was quite unmoved by the shrill voice of the farmer's wife when she called after her husband, "Mind, John, whatever you do, don't forget the saffron[4] and a penn'orth of Christmas[5]"; he never even started when the man wrenched the faggots from the furze-rick, though he sang the Flora[6] tune to words of his own composition, as he pulled at the stems. Three loads of faggots the man bore to the house, the low sun which caught the ridge of the barn and cote bathing his face as he went past the farmyard gate. In the quiet that reigned when at last the kitchen door closed for the night behind him the hare dropped to the yard, where he picked up every blade of hay he could find before leaving for his round.

Rarely had he been at a greater loss to know where to go; it was of no use seeking the moor, nothing but the unpalatable bark of withy and alder awaited him there, the fields with their scant herbage were out of his reach, High Down was inaccessible since the last snowfall; so without a goal to make for, he loped along the bridle-track, where at least the going was easy, and food, such as it was, to be had in the furze that bordered it. He was in hard case, yet not so hard as that of the predatory creatures who nightly ravaged the country and often returned supperless to their lairs. The hare knew of their forays from the trails. He had crossed two on his way back from the Down; this very night he leapt the burning line of a stoat-pack just before turning aside whilst the farmer rode past. Close to Crowz-an-Wra he stopped to browse on the bushes, standing on his hind legs and reaching as high as he could to get at the tender shoots.

Eager, however, as he was to satisfy his hunger, he was alive to everything around, and kept pricking his ears at the noise of the merriment from the cottages with windows all aglow from turnip lantern, rushlight, and the blaze of furze fire. For Crowz-an-Wra was keeping Christmas Eve with its customary cheer, little dreaming of the lonely stranger at their doors. At his slowest pace the hare passed through the village; he was no more alarmed by the illumination of the cottages than by the splendour of the heaven.

Just beyond the milestone he frisked and frolicked, and in the same high spirits galloped along the track as far as the granite cross, where, in his leverethood, he had scampered up and down the then dusty way under the eyes of his mother. At the cross he stood and listened as he had listened then, but there was not a sound; even the little stream had been frozen into silence. So he fell to rolling on the crisp surface, which crackled under him; then jumping to his feet, he scratched a pit in the snow simply to get rid of the energy which the nip in the air had excited. About midnight he galloped off through the deep snow at a pace that was surprisingly rapid, considering the weight of the snow that clung to his fur. Soon he was out of sight.

Four hours later he repassed the cross on his way home. The heavens were as resplendent as ever; Orion showed no sign of fading, the Milky Way was still a path of splendour, but the hamlet lay in gloom, and save for the rocking of a cradle, was as silent as the hills. In the homestead there was not a sound, and as if afraid to disturb the quiet, the hare stole noiselessly as a ghost to the form, where he sat watching for the dawn without a thought of sinister intrusion on the yard.

Yet he had not been there long when the cruel head of a polecat showed at the far corner by the pigsty, whence it surveyed the enclosure. She had not come for prey, she had come for shelter, and her keen eyes were peering here, there, and everywhere to see that the coast was clear before she tried to reach the retreat that had taken her fancy. Presently she galloped past the door of the cattle-house and made her way to the top of the barn steps. There she stood looking for a way in, and descrying a hole in the shutter, she scrambled up and aslant the mud wall till she gained it and squeezed through. She had not long disappeared, however, when to the amazement of the hare, her head was suddenly thrust through the snow covering the thatch, and the next instant she was hurrying over the white surface to enter the pigeon-cote. Now the cote was the home of an owl. Scarcely had the polecat curled up in it when the bird alighted on the sill, discovered the intruder, and made such a to-do that the polecat at once came out lest man's notice should be attracted, her presence revealed, and—the dread of her life—hue and cry raised. In the circumstances she was for peace at any price. Dashing past the owl she made down the roof to the hole in the thatch, where she struggled for some time to get through. At last as the result of a desperate effort she forced a passage to the barn, and so reached the yard by the way she came. From the foot of the steps she headed for the narrow passage by which she had entered, but, instead of following it, she skirted the pigsty, the poultry-houses and the open shed, with the intention of crossing the wall to the turf-rick which she had noticed from the roof. She reached the wall and was about to climb it when the latch of the kitchen door lifted. At the sound she abandoned her purpose, and that very unwisely, because she was in quite as much danger of being seen as if she had crossed the wall. For where was she to hide? There was the open shed, it is true, but she could hardly hope to gain it before the man reached the yard. "Crunch, crunch, crunch," sounded the snow under his feet; he was already close to the gate, discovery was imminent. In desperation, the bewildered creature dived into a hole in the snow made by a hoof of one of the yearlings. Even then her tail was exposed for some seconds before she succeeded in worming a way out of sight, but it did not catch the eye of the man, and for the time at least she was safe.

The hare, who had observed every movement of the polecat, kept a close watch on the spot, for he greatly feared that the creature would cross the wall at the first opportunity and perhaps discover him.

Meanwhile the hind busied himself about his ordinary duties until near noon, when he began to remove the snow from the front door, a sure sign that guests were expected. As he shovelled, he sang:

> "I saw dree ships come sailing in,
>
> Sailing in, come sailing in,
>
> I saw dree ships come sailing in,
>
> On Christmas Day in the morning"—

shovelling and singing till the steps and the path all the way to the gate were clear. No sooner had he finished than the farmer's three sons arrived, with their wives and families, the women riding pillion behind their husbands, and the children in panniers borne by donkeys. There was quite a string of donkeys; the headgear of each and of the little foal which closed the procession, was decked with holly; the merry voices of the laughing, chattering children rang out most musically. Last of all came the fiddler, a long, lean man, shivering in his thin garments as he ran, his nose blue with cold, his violin in a green baize bag under his arm. He threw a snowball at Andrew, then skipped up the steps like a lamplighter, and as the door closed on the heels of his cloth boots, it shut in the welcome with which the children greeted his arrival.

Now the work that Andrew got through between the coming of the fiddler and two of the clock, in order not to be "worried" whilst at meat, was a record on Brea Farm. In the multitude of his duties, however, one thing escaped him—he forgot to shut up the rooster. The oversight, as things turned out, meant a sore trial for the cock, tragic consequences for the hare. Nor were they long in coming.

At a few minutes past three the long snout, yellow eyes, and red tongue of Grey Fox appeared round the very corner where the polecat had showed. Whilst lying in the brake, he had heard the cock crow, and with his mate had come after it. They had come as fast as they could lay pad to ground; they were starving. For three days they had found nothing to eat over the miles and miles of country they had searched, and now at last within four leaps, there stood this fat rooster scratching away the snow. Was ever so tempting a morsel, ever so easy a victim, exposed to the eyes of ravenous wildlings? Yet the unusual silence excited Grey Fox's suspicions of a trap. Might not the bird be a bait, a decoy to lure him into the gin where he had already left one of his claws? If not, what was cock-a-doodle doing there alone? After all it was too great a risk.

But by this the little vixen—she looked but half the size of her mate—who at first kept at his brush, had come more and more forward till her mask was side by side with his. Did she by whisper or sign of eye or lip banish his scruples, goad him into action? We do not know. But the next instant he launched himself towards chanticleer, who saw him coming and raised cries so penetrating that they caused the hind and the fiddler to drop knife and fork and rush to the yard. Grey Fox had just seized the cock when the fiddler burst out, and making the most of his long legs, succeeded in heading him from the passage that led to the moor. The fox refused to drop his prey, though the huge wings kept flapping in his face and hindering him in the race with the fiddler, who pursued him over the dungheap and around the yard, to the amusement of the rest of the party crowding the gateway. As he ran, the fiddler trod on the polecat, whose sudden appearance so startled the fox that he dropped the cock, crossed the wall to the rickyard, and rejoined his mate, who had hurried away to the moor at the first shout of the fiddler.

Merry as the party was before, it was twice as merry now, yet there was not a child, nay, nor a grown-up around that festive board, who would not have been sorry to know that in the act of crossing the wall Grey Fox had espied the hare and was already plotting his destruction.

For in the earth amidst the furze, Grey Fox, who had an old score to settle, and the vixen, who had searched for him when a helpless leveret, sat mask to mask, with wrinkled brow, scheming how they should take him. It was a matter of life or death to them, at least so they themselves regarded it; and the moment their plans were laid they were all eagerness to put them into execution. Their eyes glowed with excitement; twice they rose and went to the mouth of the earth to observe the light; the third time they stole away to the rickyard.

On reaching the wall, Grey Fox peeped over, and turning his head slowly to avoid attracting notice, exchanged looks with the vixen. "It's all right, she is in the seat," that is what his glance conveyed. As the light faded he got on the wall, and watched as he crouched. Later the vixen took his place whilst he stole round to the other end of the wall. The hare was now between them, knowing all, and taking counsel with himself. From time to time the sound of the fiddle or the laughter of the children broke the tense silence, but without disquieting the foxes, who lay with their heads towards the yard ready to spring the moment the hare made off. Then the hind came and saw to the cattle, and as he presently returned to the house, hare and foxes gathered themselves for the work before them.

With a mighty bound the hare reached the yard and made for the gate, through which he passed to the front of the house with the foxes in close pursuit. The light from the window fell on the fleeting forms of all three as they rounded the corner by the beehives on their way back to the bridle-track, which the hare followed to the point where it bends. There, instead of swinging round in the direction of the hamlet, he set his face straight for Chapel Carn Brea.

Now, as at all times, he looked to the hill to escape his pursuers, but it was no longer the familiar place it had been, for the pits filled by the snow were level with the runways. Consequently the surface was treacherous, and therein lay the hope of the foxes, a hope immediately realised. Twice during the ascent the hare fell into blind holes, from which he managed to extricate himself only just in time to avoid being seized by Grey Fox. Though he escaped capture he lost the lead he had gained; abreast of the chantry he was so dangerously close to his pursuers that a false step would have meant death, and he knew it; while the foxes, who knew it too, were already anticipating a feast. For thirty yards farther the ground beneath the snow was so broken, so full of pitfalls, that the chances of traversing it without stumbling were small, but the hare got over it without mishap and reached the ridge, along which he held bravely, for the going there was good. His heart sank, however, at sight of the snow in the hollow, where only a rush or two showed above the smooth surface. But those few rushes served as a guide, a welcome guide, for they indicated the position of the Liddens, towards which he at once directed his steps.

In this he was wise, because the ice afforded reliable foothold to his hairy pads and enabled him to plough his way through the snow at quite a good pace, much faster indeed than the foxes, though they kept along the furrow in his wake. The lead thus gained he kept on increasing as he ascended Bartinney, to the discomfiture of his pursuers, who would have abandoned the chase had not the big drift in the next hollow, which they believed impassable, encouraged them to keep going. On reaching it the hare's courage failed him, and no wonder, for stretching from foothill to foothill, and completely filling the dip between, lay like a great white lake, a drift which threatened to overwhelm him. Face to face with this new danger he forgot the foxes for a moment, but the instant he looked back and caught sight of them bounding down the hill, he flung aside his hesitation, plunged into the drift, and put forth all the strength of his limbs in an effort to reach the other side. Nearer and nearer the foxes came to the drift; they leapt into it without flinching, and began to battle with the feathery mass, striving to overhaul the hare now some dozen yards ahead. It was a weird scene, that drift amidst the hills, marked now by the glowing eyes of three protruding heads, now by the tips of the ears, now only by a slight flurry of the surface, which showed where pursuers and pursued struggled beneath, till, where the snow lay deepest, there was no slightest sign of movement, and it seemed as if all three had found a grave. At last towards the farther side the points of two ears showed, then two eyes; they were the ears and eyes of the hare, who had tunnelled his way thus far, and was standing on his hind legs looking round to see where he was. Before you could count three the head was withdrawn and the hare again lost to sight, but presently out he came from the drift with a long leap, the snow on his back shooting forward between his ears as his fore feet struck the ground. He bounded up the slope, and had gone perhaps a score yards when the foxes emerged, pressing after him at their best pace. The struggle with the drift had told more on the hare than on them. Between the drift and Caer Bran, where he passed close to the spot on which months before he had sat dreaming of the life before him, he actually lost ground, yet, though seemingly doomed, on, on he sped; nay, more, he even began to gather his strength for a supreme effort to shake off his pursuers. The wood on the Beacon was the place he chose for it. The moment he felt the pine-needles under his pads he breasted the hill with the speed of the wind, and gained its granite crown several seconds ahead.

R. H. Preston & Sons, Penzance.] [*To face p. 152.*

THE REMAINS OF THE BEACON WOOD.

This spurt amazed the foxes, for they imagined the hare to be failing, and they would have been still more amazed had they known how he was using his advantage. He did not keep on as the foxes themselves would have done, for that he thought would only prolong the chase, whereas his intention was to put an end to it. So just over the ridge he leapt from rock to rock and back again, then to the great slab that looks like a vast table amidst the furze, and finally into the furze itself, into which he flung himself just in the nick of time, the bushes closing over him as Grey Fox appeared on the apex of the Beacon.

With swift glances Reynard swept the hillside, but not a spray stirred to mark the line along which their escaping prey was stealing towards the foot of the hill; forthwith he and his mate, who had now come up, stooped again to the scent with the object of following the trail. But the hare had succeeded in foiling his line; they immediately discovered the hopelessness of the task, and both returned to the high rock conscious that their only chance lay in sighting the hare as he left the hill.

Their movements had been as quick as lightning, so quick that not more than ten seconds had passed since Grey Fox gained the Beacon. How his flanks heaved, how quick the breath came from him, yet despite distress of lung and agony of lacerated pads that stained the snow with blood, his one thought was for the game; he did not waste a glance on the lanterns[7] illuminating the church tower, he was deaf to the carol-singers, all his senses were in the eyes that watched every opening between the bushes, every avenue of escape.

Suddenly, they—for the vixen was at his side—sighted the hare as it crossed the bridge far below. Instantly they were off. Twice Grey Fox tumbled head over heels in his mad haste, but the shaking made no difference to him: there was no slackening in the speed with which he led along the trail which presently recrossed the stream to a plantation. Here, in their excitement, first he then the vixen gave tongue on the scent. Their sharp yaps fell like a death-knell on the ears of the hare, who, believing the pursuit was at an end, was loping leisurely along the bank of the stream. For a moment his heart sank within him, but only for a moment; the next he pulled himself together and redoubled his pace, the thought of being seized and gobbled up by Grey Fox acting like a spur on his flagging energies. At a bound he again recrossed the stream, sped across the slope of the opposite hill in full view of the foxes and headed for a gap at the top.

The pursuers' plan was formed at once: they would waylay him at the gap and seize him as he passed. A hedge with a ditch on its further side ran up the hill. At their utmost speed the two foxes galloped along the ditch, gained the crest and reached the gap whilst the unsuspecting prey was yet a dozen yards from it. The fate of the hare was apparently sealed. But Grey Fox was not content to trust his ears to apprise him of the hare's approach; in his eagerness he could not resist peeping round the corner. This betrayed him: the hare saw his long snout, turned and made down the hill, the breathless foxes following as fast as they could. In the descent the hare gained quite a good lead, but it seemed all to no purpose, for his line of flight was leading him directly towards a quarry which cut off all escape.

Yet on he galloped straight to the brink, and reaching it, leapt headlong into the great drift that rose half-way up its sheer wall.

The foxes checked themselves on the very verge and stood gazing at the snow marked by the cleanly-cut hole made by the hare as he fell. "Done after all," was the meaning of the expression on Grey Fox's mask. But he was not to be thus deprived of his prey if search could avail, and to this end he and the vixen made their way down to the base of the quarry and were lost to sight in the drift as they worked towards the spot where they expected to find the hare lying dead.

Far from being dead, however, he was not even disabled; indeed he was none the worse for his dive, the snow having completely broken his fall. On feeling the ground beneath his pads he moved forward, and had advanced some twelve yards when he found himself confronted by the huge heap of loose rock which the quarrymen had piled there. It barred his way, threatening to prevent his escape, until presently he found a small opening, and through it squeezed to a narrow tunnel-like passage which led to a chamber littered with the remains of rabbits, mice, eels, and frogs. It was a polecat's den—the den, indeed, of the polecat that had chased him, the den where she and her kittens had slept after the pursuit. He crossed the foul lair and tried to pass through the narrow space between two rocks on the farther side. This looked like courting destruction, for he ran the risk of being jammed and unable to extricate himself; but he could hear the foxes behind him; he must go that way or perish. With a struggle he forced his head and shoulders through; then he was fixed, he could not clear his hindquarters, tug and strain as he might. As he stopped to recover his breath, he caught the patter of his pursuers' pads: they were approaching the den: in a few seconds Grey Fox's jaws would close on him and the rocks ring with his death squeal. Frantic with fear, maddened by dread of his fate, he made a frenzied effort and just managed to pull his long hind legs through before Grey Fox could seize them.

Yet to that very opening which had all but proved his destruction, he was now to owe his life. For Grey Fox, desperately anxious to reach him, forced his great head through the hole with the hope of seizing him, and got it so firmly wedged that some minutes elapsed before he succeeded in withdrawing it. By that time the hare was once more well on his way up the hill. He had passed over the brow before the foxes discovered the line of his retreat. But it was soon evident, from their half-hearted manner, that they were on the point of abandoning the pursuit, which they did a bow-shot beyond the lighted cottage.

What a change had come over them! They hardly looked the same creatures as when, alive in every fibre, they had stood on the Beacon, the embodiment of eagerness and energy. Now their heads drooped, their brushes that had waved like feathers, dragged and seemed to weigh them down. They looked dispirited, as indeed they were, and humbled too: the grass-feeder had proved more than a match for both of them, though, as they had seen, he was hampered by large balls of snow that clung to his fur. They went back the way they had come, the vixen leading, Grey Fox hopping on three legs. Twice he stopped to scratch his aching jaws, and at the bend by the quarry he disappeared from view.

The hunt was over, but even when satisfied of that the hare still held on. He was harassed now by a fresh fear, the fear of being tracked. This possessed him so strongly, that weary as he was, he wandered in and out the patches of scattered furze, confusing his trail so as to baffle any enemy who should try to trace him, and not until the long night was giving way to dawn did he settle in his form, which he sought in the old spot on the bank of the mill-pool.

That day, whilst the Squire was abroad after woodcock, he came on the triple trail above the quarry, and recognising the track of the hare, was at once filled with desire to see the end of the story told on the snow. His excitement, as he stood on the lip of the quarry, looking at the shaft-like hole, astonished his henchman: the feeling he displayed when he discovered the track of the hare by the cottage door was altogether beyond the man's comprehension.

"Ah, that shows how sorely the poor thing was pressed. Had the door been open, she would have gone in and taken her chance."

At every stride he expected to come on the end of the tragic chase, and kept looking ahead for the remains that would mark the last scene. All the greater, then, was his delight to find that the foxes had withdrawn from the chase, and greater too his determination to try and get a view of the animal whose survival in that vermin-haunted district seemed little short of miraculous. For three hours he followed the trail, pondering as he went over the animal's hairbreadth escapes as his imagination called them up and, in his anxiety to come on the hare before dusk, almost losing his temper at the delays the creature's ruses caused him. "Give it up, Squire," said his man at last; "you'll never come up with her, take and give it up."

"Not whilst there's light to see by," was the laconic reply. It was nearly four o'clock when they came to the mill-pool. Even then they searched and searched in vain, for as the hare had landed from his last spring the snow fell from the tuft and concealed him. "She's here, I know she's here," said the Squire in despair. The words were scarcely out of his mouth when the hare bounded from his feet and crossed the pond.

"Shoot, shoot," shouted the man; "darn 'ee, shoot." Instead of raising his gun, the Squire raised his hand and kept it at the salute till the creature passed from sight. It was his way of paying homage to an animal hero.

---

[4] Saffron is much used in Cornwall for colouring cakes.

[5] A pennyworth of holly.

[6] On Flora day, the 8th of May, dancing takes place in the streets of Helston.

[7] It was formerly the custom to illuminate the church towers on Christmas Day.

CHAPTER X
THE FIENDS OF THE WILD

Unrelenting as the frost seemed on Christmas Day, it yielded the next night but one to a warm westerly wind, the thaw setting in before dawn. When Andrew crossed to the bullock-house, water was dripping from the barn, by noon bush and boulder were beginning to show on the hill, at nightfall runnel and stream were chattering along their courses. The sound of running water cheered the birds at roost on branch and spray; it cheered the hare too, who kept snuffing the warm breeze that relaxed the icy fetters on the stream and melted the snow clogging his fur. Within forty-eight hours the balls of snow had completely disappeared, leaving him as light as a feather for his gallop over the moorland, where his path was marked by the spray which he spurned from the shallow pools. The splashes seemed to be caused by some ricochetting missile, so fleet were his movements: surely in all his life he never sped more swiftly than then.

But though he revelled in the exercise of his unencumbered limbs, he had a keen eye to his safety: the most wily of hunted creatures could not have been more alert and vigilant than he. Once from the solitary rock, again and again from knoll and barrow he surveyed the waste to learn whether any enemies were in sight, for he was well aware of their famished condition, and understood that they would employ the greatest stealth in attempting his capture. He kept a sharp look-out for Grey Fox, carefully examining every object that excited his least suspicion, and in his great dread of a stoat pack he repeatedly scrutinised the surface for the sinuous living line that would apprise him of its approach.

Once he thought he detected the eerie serpentine movement characteristic of the stoat; but he was mistaken, the three packs which infested his beats were miles away at the time. Though all were terrible scourges to the animals that supplied them with blood, the most formidable, on account of the sagacity and endurance of its leader, was the pack, numbering fourteen in all, whose main stronghold was the Lamorna cliffs. Even this pack was in peril of famine because of the wariness and scarcity of prey.

In their straits they invaded the homesteads, and on the fourth day of the thaw, when the ice in the pools was the last vestige of the frost, the starving brutes came pouring over the wall of Brea farmyard and made straight for the poultry-houses.

Some sought the door of the fowls' house, causing the rooster to shift uneasily on his perch; the rest circled the ducks' house without finding a way in, for Andrew had stopped the holes in the floor to which they penetrated.

Thus baulked they entered the cattle-sheds and barn, where in the dead silence they could be heard rustling among the straw. Presently a rat appeared on the roof and climbed to the old weather-cock on the roof of the pigeon-cote. Two stoats followed, but failed to trace him to the forlorn refuge whence he was watching them.

Half an hour passed thus in profitless search before the leader, standing in the middle of the yard, uttered a shrill cry. This rallied the band to her, and the yard at once seemed alive with the restless creatures darting hither and thither in their impatience to be gone.

Douglas English.]   [*To face p. 162.*

A STOAT.

They took little notice of the owl that glided to and fro, screaming as it flew; yet they were so ravenous that they would have killed and eaten him, if they could have caught him, bird of prey though he was. The farmer's wife lay awake wondering what ailed the screech-owl: the hare in the field bordering the bridle-track also wondered, but like the woman, without surmising the cause. The noise ceased when presently the pack left the yard and made past the sycamore towards the lane, seemingly on the way to the "curlew" moor. When abreast of the broken grindstone, however, the leader, who was at her wits' end to know where to go, suddenly turned and retraced her steps along the bridle-track. Abrupt as was her turning movement each stoat kept its place as though it were part of a snake, which in truth the long file closely resembled.

Reaching the stone steps into the field where the hare was at pasture, the leader appeared to be in two minds as to whether she should mount them or go straight on. A hedgehog brought her to a decision. He had been drawn from his winter quarters by the open weather, showed just then on the path and instantly attracted her. He was very sleepy, but he saw the stoats coming, immediately curled into a ball, and so awaited their onset.

What savagery the famished creatures exhibited! What determined though futile efforts they made to penetrate the hedgehog's defence! Blood was drawn, it is true, their heads were smeared with it, but it was their own blood which they licked before again falling tooth and nail on the prickly ball. Their second assault proving as unsuccessful as the first, they formed a ring around the urchin, chattering to unnerve it and so cause it to unfold. All their efforts were vain, the hedgehog was impregnable to moral as to physical attack.

But though the blood-curdling chorus was wasted on the hedgehog, it so affrighted the hare that he broke into a panic-stricken flight, nor did he stop till he had reached the chantry. There he stood listening for the cry he dreaded. His apprehensions however were unwarranted, the stoats were ignorant of his neighbourhood, and on abandoning the hedgehog retreated in the direction of the southern cliffs, slowly at first but more quickly as the night grew old, for fear of being surprised by dawn.

A faint glow suffused the low east when they reached Carn Boscawen, proceeded singly along ledge after ledge to its sea-washed face, clambered between the breaking waves up and up the wet rock and finally crept into crevices beyond reach of the spray.

For a while not a hair of them was to be seen, but the moment the sun rose they appeared at the mouths of the stronghold and lay with their long, gaunt bodies stretched to their full length to catch what little warmth the lurid orb vouchsafed.

In the light of day these night marauders looked the cruel, bloodthirsty bandits they were, the three whom the spell of Arctic cold had ermined presenting an even more fiendish aspect than the others. When too the sun passed behind the angry clouds so that carn and sea, shorn of the rays that gilded them, lay in deep shadow, the outlawed crew seemed to be in harmony with their savage surroundings and no unfit neighbours of the kite perched on the crag above.

By and by, suddenly as they had appeared, they withdrew, curled up on the rocky floor and fell asleep.

What a contrast the hare in his seat on the hill furnished to the carnivorous bandits of the carn! He looked as fearful as they looked bold, his long, quivering ears proclaimed his timidity no less plainly than the prominent eyes that overlooked the moor all the grey afternoon till they turned towards a storm far out at sea where lightning played in a black cloud, below which presently the blood-red sun went down.

And thus was ushered in a night of tragedy with hare and stoats for actors, moor and cliff for setting.

At dusk the hare left his couch and descended the hill to his pasture on Brea Farm. There he wandered from enclosure to enclosure picking up what little herbage he could find. It took him hours to get his fill.

Meanwhile the stoats who had quitted their fastness were heading for the moor, tempted by the presence of some wading birds which they had disturbed the previous night on their return journey. On the way they turned aside here and there in the hope of securing other prey, so that it was within an hour of midnight when they reached the purlieus of the waste, that looked pitch-black beneath the stormy sky.

At the spot where they struck the heath they were two miles from the linhay field which the hare presently left for his usual gallop. So wide however was its surface that nine times out of ten the pack might have hunted and the hare enjoyed his spin without either being aware of the other's presence; twice it had so happened during the month now within an hour of its close; but the hare's good fortune had temporarily forsaken him and his time come to stand before the pack.

Black though the night was, had the hare been as alert as usual, he could hardly have failed to discern at least the ghostly forms of the white members of the band in time to secure a long start and perhaps get clean away. Immunity from molestation in the moor explains the poor look-out he kept. His lack of vigilance was to cost him dear, inasmuch as he succeeded in arresting his steps only just in time to avoid running into the pack as it showed above the slight rise that for a few seconds had effectually concealed it from view.

At sight of them he turned and fled, and though more frightened than ever before, did the best thing possible; he made straight for the pool, for he hoped by placing the wide water between him and his pursuers to disconcert them and put an end to the chase.

The stoats followed, forging ahead at their utmost pace, except when they checked their steps and stood still to look about them as is their wont; why, it is impossible to say, but certainly not to give "law" to the quarry. So several seconds ahead of them, the hare reached the pool midway between the islet and the reed-bed, plunged in, floundered through the shallows, and on getting beyond his depth, struck out for the opposite shore.

Ice still covered most of the surface, but following an open channel he got more than half-way across before he found himself confronted by a sheet which, thin and rotten though it was, arrested his progress.

He tried to clamber on to it but the brittle edge broke under his pads. His position was most critical. To make matters worse, the cry of his pursuers now sounded very distinct; they were evidently close to the pool. What if they took to the water and met him as he swam? For he must go back or drown. In the dilemma he turned and struck out for the shore he had left. He seemed to be swimming into the jaws of death. Soon however fortune befriended him. For as he swam he saw at one side a narrow strait just wide enough to admit him, and into it he turned as the pack took to the water, swimming swiftly and with heads held high. They must have viewed the hare had not the moon been completely obscured by a black cloud, which completely shut off the pallid beams that for a brief space had lit the moor.

Soon they passed the narrow opening and approached the barrier. No barrier did it prove to them. They landed with the greatest ease, galloped over the ice, gained the shore and began casting for the quarry. Meanwhile the hare had gained the reed-bed whence, owing to the conspicuousness of the ermined stoats, he was able to follow the movements of the pack, till presently the ghostly forms were swallowed up in the darkness as they made for the further end of the pool.

The hare seizing the opportunity made off, his face set for the "curlew" moor. No longer however does he move with full freedom of limb; the paralysing influence of the stoats is upon him. How he labours as if held back by some restraining hand, how slow his progress! He feels doomed, for escape is impossible and refuge there is none.

Suddenly he stops, as suddenly resumes his way, but in a direction at right angles to his former course.

Across the black waste he has seen the glimmer of light that tells of the presence of man. He is making towards it as to a beacon of hope. By and by he reaches the church, from whose coloured windows the glow proceeds, and from his station amongst the tombs listens to the singing. Whilst he listens there comes from the moor the shrill cry of his pursuers. At the sound he resumes his flight, following the rude road through the village towards Sennen Green, where he halts as if loath to quit the abode of man for the wild beyond. Death is approaching, but it must overtake him; he cannot await his fate. Whilst the bells ring the old year out, the new year in, he lopes on and on past Vellandreath, past Genvor to the lonely Tregiffian cliffs. There from a rise he looks back and sees the extended file of his enemies as they gallop down the opposite slope. The ground in front is studded with rocks. Threading his way among these he finds himself within a score yards of some men lying on the turf. As they lie they form an irregular ring. Into this he passes without an instant's hesitation and squats in their midst.

The stoats on the other hand fell to silence, stopping motionless by the rocks.

The men were smugglers and all asleep save the sentry, who lay near the edge of the cliff watching so eagerly for the expected boat that he had not heard the stoats' cry, though it sounded distinct above the roar of the sea.

R. H. Preston & Sons.]　[To face p. 170.

SENNEN CHURCH TOWER.

Presently the man rose to his feet and paced up and down, his oilskins creaking as he moved. Only for a moment did he take his eyes from the dark waters below whilst he ignited the tinder and lit his pipe. Now and again a spark was blown in the direction of the stoats, but they took no more notice of that than of the cry uttered by one of the sleeping smugglers. Nothing would drive the bold, ravenous pack away, at least nothing but dawn; and that was hours and hours distant.

Suddenly a red light came and went near the foot of the cliffs; it was a signal from the boat and was answered by the watch with a hoot like that of a screech-owl. Immediately all was stir, the men jumping to their feet and making for the adit that communicated with the cave into which the boat with its load of kegs had already been taken.

The hare, far from being frightened by the sudden commotion, dogged the steps of the men and sat in a recess in the wall of the tunnel; the stoats who had followed dared not penetrate there; so they stood and watched him from the mouth.

The smugglers worked as if for their lives; two, by means of a long rope, hauling the kegs from the cave to the adit, whilst the other five carried them to the furzebrake on the hillside and hid them amongst the bushes.

The continual passing to and fro of the men cheered the hare in his niche, for it served to alarm the stoats and keep them at a distance.

Scarcely had the last of the kegs been hidden away when one of the smugglers, he who had cried out in his sleep, gave a false alarm, causing the others to rush to the adit, where one after the other they slid down the rope to the cave, all except the sentry, whose duty it was to haul up the line and stow it away. An old hand at the trade and a man of iron nerve, he proceeded to coil the rope in the most leisurely way before he came out of the adit, bringing the rope on his arm. He thought he was alone, but he was not; the hare kept as close to his heels as a dog, while the stoats followed at a short distance.

Dark though it was, the smuggler held along the brink of the cliff till compelled to swerve by a great pile of rocks that looked against the murky sky like a black wall. By and by as he skirted it he stopped and, shifting the rope to his left arm, began feeling the face of the rock with his right. He was searching for the rude steps by which he would reach the summit of the carn to hide the rope, the hare meanwhile remaining so close to his feet that once it actually grazed his sea-boots with its soft side. Presently he found the place and began the ascent, thus leaving the hare to the mercy of the stoats.

Before the smuggler had climbed four feet the hare realised his danger. At once he fled along the edge of the cliff, the stoats, who had already begun to creep towards him, in hot pursuit.

Whilst he was free from the numbing sensation of fear, which had subsided in the friendly presence of man, his relentless persecutors even at their utmost speed seemed almost motionless behind him, but the moment it returned, cramping his powers, he lost ground.

Then he began to look anxiously about him to find a refuge, as in that lay now his only hope of escape.

The sea from half a score caverns bellowed its invitation, but he heeded it not. Only in the last resort would he cast himself over the cliff, so in weariness and fear he struggled on with the terrorising cry of the pack ever in his ears.

Before him lay a small and oddly shaped headland, so narrow at its base that any animal seeking the coast beyond was certain to cross the neck and avoid going round.

Not so the hare. As if fearful of losing touch of the cliff, he took no notice of the short cut, but held on round the promontory till, near the extreme point, he struck and followed a track laid by foxes—a treacherous track, that after winding in and out between overhanging rocks and the lip of the cliff, suddenly ended on the brink of a precipice. He saw the predicament he was in shortly after rounding the point, and despair gripped his heart.

But when he had almost given himself up for lost, a shelf of rock that projected over the track offered asylum if only he could reach it. Once, twice he gathered his limbs, only to recoil from launching himself at the leap, for he felt that it was more than he could compass. Then he listened to the swelling cry; that warned him he had not a moment to lose.

Animals, like men, when face to face with death, perform feats seemingly beyond their powers. Thus it was with the hare, into whose mad spring was concentrated all the force that love of life could rouse. But his greatest efforts merely enabled him to get such a grip of the rock as prevented him from falling back. Frantic was his struggle to complete a lodgment by dragging his hind legs to the shelf. He succeeded just in time to squat as the first of the stoats came galloping round the point and pulled up at the spot where the trail suddenly ended. In a twinkling the rest of the band followed, and recognising the situation, looked to the leader for guidance.

No time was lost. Some went to the end of the track and stood gazing at the depths below, but the greater number followed the leader over the brink of the precipice, abreast of the ledge. The daring creatures seemed to be courting destruction in attempting the descent; their claw-grip and marvellous agility, however, took them safely down places that might have been thought to deny foothold, and all reached the undercliff without mishap. Now they stood at the edge of the tide, where from every point of vantage, even from the crown of the streaming rocks, they scanned the white water, appearing to imagine that the hare had leapt into the surf and was to be seen there if only their eyes could detect her. Nothing met their gaze except a splintered bowsprit, and by and by, after extending their search beyond the point, they climbed the cliff again, rejoining the others where they stood beneath the ledge.

The situation of the starving creatures was a desperate one, and for a moment the leader was as completely at a loss what to do as the rest of the pack. Suddenly it occurred to her that the hare might have returned on his trail, have leapt aside and made off inland; the next instant she sprang over the backs of the stoats surrounding her, to return to the extreme point. That was the spot from which she conjectured he would make his leap, and on reaching it she searched the ground near it for traces of his scent. Nose to ground she tried rocks, fern, cushions of sea-pinks, even the heather covering the highest part of the headland, before going back to a spot near the point where she happened to be on a level with the shelf.

At that moment the moon lit up the scene, silvering the sea, revealing the narrow track and the pack clustered there with heads directed to their leader. Her attitude tells them something has excited her curiosity. Her eyes are scrutinising the strange object on the ledge, and though it lies completely shadowed by another ledge above, she presently recognises the hare, and in some way communicates her discovery to her followers.

Thereupon they strive to reach the shelf, some by the overhanging wall, the rest by leaping; but all their efforts are in vain.

Meanwhile the leader has succeeded in gaining the higher ledge, from which by craning her neck she is able to see the hare beneath, who indeed is within a few feet of her.

The upper shelf is semicircular, and point after point of its circumference she examines in the hope of being able to get at her prey. Soon she discovers a notch. From this, twisting her lissom body, she tries to leap to the lower shelf, only to fail, and narrowly escape falling over the precipice. She is soon back for another attempt. Once and again she is near succeeding. Had the indent been a little deeper, had the under ledge projected but another inch, had it only been a little lower, she must have flung herself on to it; but as it stood, it was beyond her skill.

Her resources, however, were not exhausted. Resting her fore feet on the edge of the shelf, every toe extended and every claw gripping the rock, she lowered her long white body and swung it to and fro like a ghostly pendulum. Now this way, now that, it oscillated, till presently at the full extent of her inward swing she let go—falling on her back within a few inches of the hare.

Then he showed the wonderful grit that was in him. As she fell he rose, lashed out with his powerful hind legs and sent her flying by a kick that drove her over the edge, down, down, down to the raging waters far below.

The loss of their leader discouraged the rest of the pack. As if in distress, they kept darting up and down the track till a deluge of rain drove them off.

The hare was left master of the field. His flank rose and fell more quickly than its wont, the pupils of his eyes were distended as never before, but already he was planning his escape, and had chosen the retreat he would make for.

Hours of blinding rain followed, lightning occasionally lit up the blackness shrouding cliff and sea; it was no weather for any living thing to be abroad in, and indeed nothing appeared till near dawn, when a bedraggled white creature made her way with difficulty up the face of the cliff and staggered to the track. It was the leader of the stoats, who after struggling with the backwash which had nearly buffeted the life out of her, had managed to land, and after a long rest, come back for her followers.

Awhile she stood beneath the ledge and looked up. Too feeble to do more, she meant to return at dusk to pit her wit against the hare's, in some way to get at him, drive her fangs into his great vein and drink deep of his blood: she was even thinking of the feast in prospect as she crawled away on the trail of the pack.

She was, however, reckoning without her host. In as wild a dawn as ever broke upon the Land's End, the hare leapt from his sanctuary and stole over the rain-lashed moor to Chapel Carn Brea, where, happy in the thought that the downpour would destroy all trace of his trail, he fell soundly asleep, nor even dreamt of the terrible ordeal through which he had passed.

CHAPTER XI
L'HOMME S'AMUSE

As if to compensate the persecuted animal for his recent trials, the hare now enjoyed what was to him a long immunity from molestation, for during January and part of February no enemy waylaid or pursued him.

At the end of that time the weather, which had again become bleak and inclement, suddenly softened with the return of the westerly wind, becoming so mild as to savour of spring. The change was felt and responded to by every creature. On St Valentine's Day when Golden Valley resounded with the love songs of birds, the hare had already set out in search of a mate. Whether influenced by reason or by instinct, he did not seek her along his usual beats, on which he had not once crossed the trail of his kind, but set his face to the north, to the unexplored land he had often looked down on from Bartinney and Chapel Carn Brea; there he was in high hope of meeting her.

So intent was he on his quest that he never stopped to browse, leaving untouched patch after patch of tender herbage in the moorland farms he crossed. Yet he never saw a living thing. He came to the wild which is crowned by the weird rocks of Carn Kenidzhek, and here, standing near the summit, he scrutinised the moonlit waste, apparently a desolate land, a land without life. Just before daybreak, however, there came into view, ghostly as the stoats but very much larger, a creature threading its way in and out among the furze bushes as it made for the Carn. The hare was puzzled as to its identity until it began to ascend the slope, when to his surprise he saw that it was that uncommon thing, a white badger.

It presently winded the hare, stood, gazed at him, then after a glance at the faint glow in the depressions between the hills, hurried to its earth. As soon as it had disappeared the hare sought a couch in the heather, and sat with his face to the far-off Carns, whose crests were soon bright in the rays of the rising sun.

"In that golden land," he thought, "I shall surely find her. To-night I will go there."

The day proved as glorious as the night had been serene, but for the hare it was all too long. He could hardly sit in his form, so eager was he to be afoot, and the moment the stars peeped he quitted the seat.

What miles on miles he traversed: he visited the hills, he penetrated to the cliffs of Morvah, he turned inland again and roamed wide stretches of moor and down, he skirted Chun[8] cromlech, and passed within sight of the Men Scryfa as he headed for the Galver, with its upthrust peak conspicuous against the stars. From the Galver he went to Hannibal's Carn, and presently stood on its highest rock gazing at the plain beneath. His ears were pricked as they had been a score times since sundown to catch the whispers of the waste and perhaps hear the bleat of a doe. He listened as he had never listened before; but there came no call, no sound indeed save the murmur of the dawn wind about the crags; so at last the love-sick fellow forsook his station and returned to the Galver, where after weaving a maze of trails he sought a form high up the slope.

In his lone retreat he felt as safe as on Chapel Carn Brea; he was even more remote from the haunts of man. Yet harriers were already on their way to the meet, and it was that very ground where he sat that was to be hunted.

The Squire of Trengwainton had breakfasted by candlelight, and as the clock over the stables was striking half-past six, he mounted his favourite grey mare and started out attired in full hunting costume, green coat, white breeches, boots reaching almost to the knee, and a velvet cap that well became his clean-shaven face. Twelve couple of hounds followed at his horse's heels, the little procession as it made its way along the avenue of beeches being closed by Sam Noy, the whipper-in.

Coming to the high ground beyond the Forest Carn where the track forks, the squire turned in his saddle and asked which road he should take.

"The lower road, Sir Tudor," was the prompt reply. Strange though it seems that the Squire of Trengwainton should ask his way to the meet, the explanation is simple.

He had arrived in Cornwall from Pembroke only three weeks earlier, after a voyage exciting even for those disturbed times. The schooner in which he sailed was attacked off the Land's End by a privateer which had been harassing St Ives, and compelled to run before the wind in order to escape capture. Under cover of darkness she got away, and reached St Ives with no more damage than a hole in her mainsail and the loss of her topmast. But the mayor and the watch mistaking the rakish-looking craft for another Frenchman, had opened fire from the three four-pounders on the "Island"—luckily without effect, the balls dropping at least fifty yards short.

The incident had so greatly amused the squire that the very memory of it brought a smile to his face again and again as he rode through the grey dawn. By and by the sun rose, making a jewel of every dewdrop, and calling forth the carols of the birds.

This changed the train of his thoughts. His mind reverted to Gaston de Foix, of all followers of the chase the one dearest to his heart, and after passing the farmhouse at Lanyon as he descended the hill to the millpool he was quoting aloud: "Et quant le soleil sera levé, il verra celle douce rosée sur rincelles et herbettes et le soleil par sa vertu les fera reluysir. C'est grant plaisance et joye au cœur du veneur."

"We turn in here, sir," presently interposed the whipper-in, who thought the squire had taken leave of his seven senses.

"Four Parishes, where the meet is, lies right afore 'ee under the Galver, and the Galver is that git hill up again' the sky theere."

Whereupon Sir Tudor left the track for the moor lined with the shadows of the Carns.

Awaiting him at Four Parishes[9] were Squire Tregenna, to whose gun-fire he had been exposed in St Ives Bay, Squire Praed of Trevethoe, a few yeomen, some crofters for the most part fairly mounted, and a promiscuous crowd of men afoot, amongst whom the fiddler's pinched face peeped out between the rough beards of two tall smugglers, and three or four ne'er-do-wells were marked off by their careless slouch from the sturdier forms of half a dozen miners.

After greetings had been exchanged, Sir Tudor appealed to Jim Curnow of Towednack, whose keenness and knowledge he had already noticed: "Where shall we draw first?"

"Try the ground about the Galver," said Curnow, "if there's a hare left in the country she'll be there."

So it was decided; and all moved off to the hill, where the pack scattered freely in search of the game.

They were a level lot of hounds, very much alike to a stranger, yet as different in the eyes of the squire as were their names to his ears. He had named them himself, most happily Squire Praed thought, on hearing Sir Tudor call in turn on Melody, Corisande, Guinevere, Merlin, Cymro, and Caradoc.

Awhile each hound worked separately, indifferent to all around, one would have thought, yet in reality keenly observant of the others, for as soon as Trueboy waved his stern half a score flocked to him.

They are at once all excitement, as well they may be; they have hit the line of the hare, and are following it between the two big boulders where he passed on his way to Hannibal's Carn, the tan splashes on their coats gleaming like russet gold in the slant sunlight, their musical voices awakening the echoes of the rocks, and thrilling every member of the little field.

Soon they return to the Galver, clinging tenaciously to the trail, whose bewildering maze they strive their utmost to unravel. The eager movements of every hound show that he knows the hare is near and will soon be afoot, yet, when like a shadow gliding over the sunlit slope below the ridge he silently steals away, not one even suspects that he has risen, much less catches a glimpse of his crouching form.

The squire, however, has viewed him; his hand proclaims it, raised to command silence and allow a reasonable start to the jack, who still moves stealthily in the hope of getting away unobserved. But the moment the squire cheers the hounds on to his line he knows that he has been seen, instantly abandons his slinking tactics and breaks into a gallop, his head pointed straight for his native hills.

It was an exhilarating moment for Sir Tudor, and as he settled down to ride, what with the pleasant undulations of his horse, what with the freshness of the morning and the wildness of the country, above all with the thought that his little companions in a hundred hunts were chiming on the scent of their first Cornish hare, he would not have changed seats with King George.

He kept sufficiently close to the pack to observe the niceties of the chase and help the hounds in case of a check; but they held on, straight as a crow might fly, in the direction of Chun Castle.

There the hare stopped for the first time and looked back. His glance, which took in hounds, horsemen, and the straggling line of pedestrians, removed all doubts that he himself was the object of pursuit, so he laid his ears back again and resumed his gallop, scared nearly as much by the glaring sunlight as by the cries of the pack.

Twice he swerved, the first time to cross a ploughed field which he knew would hold little scent, and again to thread his way among the cattle in a field beyond. Presently he crossed the track to St Just close behind a train of mules bearing tin ore, set foot on Balleswidden common, and soon saw the hills of his first home right ahead of him.

Cheered by the sight he sped bravely on across the waste of furze and heather to the foothills, and bounded up the slope with a vigour that showed little sign of fatigue. He was making for the form. There he believed he would be safe when shielded by a ruse, for he meant after going nearly to the foot of Chapel Carn Brea to return on his line and leap aside into his seat.

His mind was full of his purpose as he skirted the Liddens, and a little way beyond them he stopped to satisfy himself that he had time to carry out his plan before the hounds came up. Though he listened intently, he heard nothing; his pursuers had been delayed in the ploughed field as he expected: he had ample opportunity for his manœuvre.

Yet the whole plan came to nought. On reaching the chantry he suddenly leapt aside as if from an ambuscade, for he found himself in the presence of man. There on a rock sat an antiquary sketching the ruin, and so engrossed by his task that he never saw the hare. Even if he had he would not have raised a finger to scare it, much less betray its refuge to the hounds. But the hare's faith in man was gone. He fled down the hill towards Brea Farm, save for the thud of the flail in the barn silent as in winter, and from thence to the moor, over which he rather loped than galloped, for he was getting exhausted.

Meanwhile Sir Tudor had reached the chantry. Despite the excitement of the chase he reined in his mare, and looked for the first time on Cornwall's fairest scene.

"Fine subject for a canvas," he said, addressing the antiquary.

"Yes, but not half so impressive as this old oratory, with its memories."

"Perhaps you are right," said the squire, riding on again after the hounds, now streaming over the boundary wall.

The mare took him over the wall with the greatest ease, and soon was cantering along the bridle-track, watched by Andrew, whom the music of the hounds had drawn to the barn steps.

"Have you seen her?" asked Sir Tudor, when he reached the farmyard.

"Seed what, sir?"

"The hare?"

"No, sir, theere ed'n such a crittur in the country."

Later the fiddler came running past. "Where are they, Andrew?" he asked breathlessly.

"Gone right over the 'curley' moor straight for Hayl Kimbra Pool. But what's the hurry? Stop and have a bit of croust,[10] a bit o' heavy cake."[11]

"Lor' bless the boy, 'tes no time for feasting nor fiddling. Did 'ee ever hear such pretty music as they little dogs give out?"

And without waiting for an answer the fiddler went off as if his life depended on being in at the finish.

Andrew had directed him well, for the hare had gone to the pool where he had his first swim. The hounds following, crossed it as if nothing could live before them; but on the far side of the moor, where beyond Trevescan it slopes gently to the sea, they were in difficulties. The hare had run along a stone wall, returned a score yards on his trail, leapt into the track it bordered, and gone off in the direction of his cliff retreat, now his goal.

There for the first time the squire came to their aid. He solved the mystery of the wall in vain, for the track held no scent, and he was face to face with defeat.

Hearing a shout, he looked up and saw a man on a bank waving his hat.

"Did you see her, my man?" said he, riding up to him.

"I did, sir, and flinged this pollack at her, and turned her."

"Was she done up?"

"Not a bit, for when I heaved the fish, she took down along over they rocks there, like a ball of fire. But if you're going down to the point, you'd better leave hoss and hounds behind. 'Tes no place for they."

Taking the hint, Sir Tudor left his mare and the hounds in charge of the whipper-in, and casting his eyes right and left as he went in the hope of seeing the hare, made his way to the extremity of the headland.

"What do you call this point?"

"Why, bless thee, I thought every grown man knowed that!"

"'Tes the Land's End."

"Ah!" ejaculated Sir Tudor reflectively. He was moved at learning that he stood at the uttermost verge of the land; for a moment he forgot all about the hare, but only for a moment.

"I hope she's not gone over," said he, as he looked down at the seething waters. Then after a pause, he added with much feeling—"She was as stout a hare as ever stood before hounds."

He quite believed that the jack had leaped over rather than be taken; but he was wrong. The distressed creature had found a sanctuary amongst the rocks, where the hounds would never have found him even had they been allowed to search.

There we will leave him, for though his after years were marked by hairbreadth escapes, his adventures do not exceed in interest those that have been chronicled.

One incident, however, must be mentioned.

Within four days of the chase he returned to Hannibal's Carn, where he found a mate worthy of his fine qualities, and for a time his happiness was complete.

All his days he remained true to his native hill; in the end he crept beneath the ruins of the chantry, and there the toad guarded the portal of his death-chamber.

---

[8] *Pron.* Choon.

[9] A spot marked by a granite post, where the parishes of Gulval, Madron, Morvah, and Zennor meet.

[10] The food taken at the meal between breakfast and dinner.

[11] A toothsome cake peculiar to Cornwall.

Milton Keynes UK
Ingram Content Group UK Ltd.
UKHW042146281024
450365UK00010B/646